FAITH AND THE FIGHT

MICHAEL WILLIAMS
FAITH AND THE FIGHT

A DETAILED GUIDE ON RECOGNIZING AND CONQUERING SPIRITUAL ATTACK IN EVERYDAY LIFE

© 2023 By Michael Williams

Published by Zoe Life Consulting Group LLC

ZOE LIFE
CONSULTING GROUP

www.zoelifeconsultinggroup.com

All rights reserved. No part of this publication may be reproduced, distributed, or transmitted in any form or by any means, including photocopying, recording, or other electronic or mechanical methods, without the prior written permission of the publisher, except in the case of brief quotations embodied in critical reviews and certain other noncommercial uses permitted by copyright law.

Although the author and publisher have made every effort to ensure that the information in this book was correct at press time, the author and publisher do not assume and hereby disclaim any liability to any party for any loss, damage, or disruption caused by errors or omissions, whether such errors or omissions result from negligence, accident, or any other cause.

Adherence to all applicable laws and regulations, including international, federal, state, and local governing professional licensing, business practices, advertising, and all other aspects of doing business in the U.S., Canada, or any other jurisdiction, is the sole responsibility of the reader and consumer.

Neither the author nor the publisher assumes any responsibility or liability whatsoever on behalf of the consumer or reader of this material. Any perceived slight of any individual or organization is purely unintentional.

The resources in this book are provided for informational purposes only and should not be used to replace the specialized training and professional judgment of a health care or mental health care professional.

Neither the author nor the publisher can be held responsible for the use of the information provided within this book. Please always consult a trained professional before making any decision regarding treatment of yourself or others.

English Bible Versions Cited

The various English Bible translations cited in this work, excluding the King James translation, are all copywritten. They are listed as follows:

NIV – Scripture quotations taken from The Holy Bible: New International Version, NIV. Copywrite 1973, 1978, 1984, 2011 by Biblica, Inc. Translated by the Committee on Bible Translation, Zondervan, 2011. Used by permission. All rights reserved.

ESV – Scripture quotations taken from The Holy Bible: English Standard Version. Crossway, 2016. Used by permission. All rights reserved.

NASB2020 – Scripture quotations taken from The Holy Bible: New American Standard Bible 2020. The Lockman Foundation, 2020. Used by permission. All rights reserved.

NLT – Scripture quotations taken from The Holy Bible: New Living Translation. Tyndale House, 2015. Used by permission. All rights reserved.

NET – Scripture quotations taken from The Holy Bible: New English Translation. Biblical Studies Press, 2005. Used by permission. All rights reserved.

NKJV – Scripture quotations taken from The Holy Bible: New King James Version. Thomas Nelson, 1982. Used by permission. All rights reserved.

ISBN: 979-8-89109-333-1 (paperback)
ISBN: 979-8-89109-425-3 (hardback)
ISBN: 979-8-89109-334-8 (ebook)
ISBN: 979-8-89109-424-6 (audio)

GET YOUR FREE GIFT
FROM ZOE LIFE CONSULTING GROUP

Sign up for our FREE *Life to the Full* newsletter! Get reflections, observations, and commentary as we dive deeper into areas of scripture, delivered to your inbox weekly.

Subscribe here! www.zoelifeconsultinggroup.com/newsletter

And to get the best experience and the most help from this book, readers are encouraged to download our companion workbook—*Faith and the Fight - A Detailed Guide on Recognizing and Conquering Spiritual Attack in Everyday Life: A Workbook for Personal Reflection and Growth*. The workbook provides additional reflections, activities, and next steps that enable the reader to implement the ideas covered in the book and move more quickly to victory in the spiritual battles that we all face.

You can get your copy by visiting
www.zoelifeconsultinggroup.com/books

For Minnie

"*We both will kick out that devil with God on our side fighting our battles.*"

CONTENTS

Introduction xi

Chapter 1: What Is Spiritual Warfare? 1
Chapter 2: Recognizing Spiritual Warfare 7
Chapter 3: Preparing Yourself for the Fight—
Union With God 18
Chapter 4: Preparing Yourself for the Fight—
Sin, Repentance, Forgiveness, and Mercy 38
Chapter 5: Preparing Yourself for the Fight—
Faith, Trust, and the Holy Spirit 61
Chapter 6: Preparing Yourself for the Fight—
Prayer and Fasting 94
Chapter 7: Preparing Yourself for the Fight—
Understanding Your Authority 107
Chapter 8: Preparing Yourself for the Fight—
The Armor of God 114
Chapter 9: Preparing Yourself for the Fight—
Understanding the Enemy 141
Chapter 10: How We Fight 156
Chapter 11: How We Fight—Fear 176
Chapter 12: How We Fight—Worry and Anxiety 183

Chapter 13:	How We Fight—Abandonment and Loneliness	190
Chapter 14:	How We Fight—Hopelessness and Despair	198
Chapter 15:	How We Fight—Confusion	208
Chapter 16:	How We Fight—Temptation	216
Chapter 17:	How We Fight—Fighting for Others	224
Chapter 18:	What to Expect	232

Acknowledgments	243
Review	245
About the Author	247
Notes	249
More	253

INTRODUCTION

Why is this happening to me?

I have asked myself that question countless times over the years, but none more than about a year ago. My mom started experiencing some health issues, and I had to leave my home and come stay with her to help care for her. And while I needed to come to stay with my mom, my wife needed to stay at home. I started noticing a feeling of distance between my wife and me. She noticed it as well. Not just the physical distance. A feeling of emotional distance. Spiritual distance. Our communication started to change. Why was my wife telling me the things she was telling me? After years together, she felt like we should separate and just remain friends. I know she loves me, and I know I love her. I then started looking at my actions and the things I was saying to her as well. My words and actions didn't reflect the love I felt for her either. We both have a strong belief in God and believe that He brought us together. It really couldn't have happened any other way, but that's another story for another time.

So, if we both love each other and both believe that God brought us together, the question kept coming up, "Why is this happening to me? Why is this happening to us? What is going on here?" This wasn't really the heart of my wife, and it wasn't the heart of me, either. Neither of us was being our true and authentic selves, but why?

And what were we experiencing? Fear. Uncertainty. Confusion. Doubt. Doubt in ourselves, doubt in each other, and when we really stopped and considered it, doubt in God. Feelings that our marriage wasn't meant to be. Feelings that our situation was hopeless. Feelings that God didn't really intend for us to be married. Not being honest with each other. And, in many cases, not being honest with ourselves.

Through lots of prayers and Bible study, I came to the realization that we do have an enemy, and the enemy wants nothing more than to destroy the good things that God intends for us. I started focusing on the possibility that this was a spiritual attack. I came to the realization that these feelings we were having were nothing but lies. Lies that our marriage wasn't meant to be. Lies that our situation was hopeless. Lies that God didn't intend for us to be married. Lies that we couldn't share things with each other. An enemy was feeding us these lies, and we had been agreeing with them. I looked back at other times when my wife and I had struggles, and again, it pointed to spiritual attacks at those times as well. The more I studied, the more I realized that there were so many areas in life where attacks were happening, and we were oblivious to it. We had no idea it was happening. But once I realized it, I knew I needed to do something. But what?

When I first talked to my wife about this, she was not only skeptical but flat-out denied it. She didn't believe it was spiritual warfare. So, I began praying on my own. I studied more. I changed the way I prayed. Then I began rebuking. I studied more. I changed the way I rebuked. When I began, there were certainly times I was discouraged. Times that it seemed hopeless. I wanted to give up, and at times, I did. But

God is so faithful! I started praying and rebuking again. Then I saw a shift in not only my life and heart but in my wife's life and heart as well. We talked about spiritual attacks again, but now, she acknowledged it. After a few more conversations, she fully believed it, and she wanted to fight it as well.

My wife and I are now fully committed to this. She and I know it happens, and we can more easily recognize it when it is happening. And we both agree, had we not recognized it for what it was and taken the steps to resist and rebuke it, we would no longer be together today. And we both recognize that it is ongoing. It is something that we don't take lightly or try to sweep under the rug and ignore. We face it head-on, together with God.

It worked for us. And if it worked for us, it can work for anyone. We are both just regular people. We didn't attend seminary. But we do now have experience. Live ammo experience under battle conditions. And we do believe had we done nothing, or had we waited, we wouldn't be together today. We were that close. It has not only helped our relationship, but we now see and recognize spiritual attack in so many areas of our lives. It has truly been a blessing to know how to recognize these attacks and fight back. To conquer. To gain back the blessings that God wants to give us. And we continually have to work to recognize them. I felt led to share the things we learned along the way in order to help others. That's why I wrote this book.

That's what this book is all about. Recognizing spiritual warfare in your everyday life and how to conquer it. You may have asked yourself the same question, "Why is this happening to me?" Consider the possibility that you are under spiritual attack.

Friends, there is hope! There is peace to be found. There is joy to be found. There is love to be found.

> "The thief comes only to steal and kill and destroy; I have come that they may have life, and have it to the full."
>
> *John 10:10 NIV*

Don't wait. Recognize the thief so you can have life and have it to the full.

CHAPTER 1

What is Spiritual Warfare?

I remember the movie *The Exorcist*[1] coming out in the early 70s when I was a kid. My family had traveled to Albuquerque, NM, with my dad on a business trip. It was an overnight stay, and we wanted to watch a family movie. *The Exorcist* was newly released, and my family knew nothing about it. When my parents asked about it at the theater, they were a little shocked. So we watched something else that night instead. But I did see it later when I was much older, and it was disturbing, to say the least. Linda Blair's head spinning around, vomiting green stuff all over the bed, her face grossly disfigured, and the creepy voice. Hollywood has given us their take on spiritual warfare. It has gone from the grotesque images in *The Exorcist* to the GQ images in the series *Lucifer*,[2] in which Lucifer, or Satan, leaves hell to go live in LA, helping police solve crimes. So, which is the correct portrayal? Biblically speaking, neither is truly accurate, although Lucifer

---

[1] *The Exorcist*, directed by William Friedkin, Warner Brothers, Hoya Productions, 1973.
[2] *Lucifer*, developed by Tom Kapinos, Jerry Bruckheimer Television, DC Entertainment, Warner Bros. Television, Netflix, 2016–2021.

comes closer in a particular way—he hides from everyone who he really is. He deceives.

To gain some perspective on what spiritual warfare actually is from a biblical perspective rather than what Hollywood has presented, we don't have to look any further than what is arguably the most well-known story of the Bible—the birth of Jesus.

The birth of Jesus is the most familiar to us, as told in the 2nd Chapter of Luke. A very pregnant Mary and her husband Joseph had traveled to Bethlehem for a census ordered by Caesar Augustus. While there, she gave birth to a son and placed Him in a manger, which is nothing more a feeding trough. The Bible tells us she did this because no guest rooms were available. They were forced to stay in a stable.

Outside Bethlehem, shepherds watched over their flocks during the night. An angel appeared to the shepherds, and the Bible tells us they were *terrified*. Most people who encounter angels in the Bible are *terrified*. Angels aren't how they are most often depicted these days—babies with wings—soft, cute, and cuddly, with a little halo floating above their head. The Bible describes different kinds of angels, but none as soft, cute, cuddly babies!

OK, back to the story. The angel tells the shepherds, "Do not be afraid," and announces the birth of the Savior, the Messiah, and tells them they will find Him in Bethlehem, wrapped in cloths and lying in a manger. Then, what is described as the "great company of the heavenly host" appears with the angel, praising God. And again, back to the shepherds being terrified, "heavenly host" refers to the army of angels. These weren't cuddly babies; these were warriors! The shepherds quickly go to Bethlehem and find the child, just as the angels told them. They left and spread the word, telling others about what the angel shared with them about this child. The shepherds then returned to their flocks, praising God for everything they had heard and seen. It is a beautiful story. And all true. But another story was also happening that night. One not seen by the shepherds. For that, let's go to the Book of Revelation.

Many may not be aware of this story of the birth of Jesus—

> *A great sign appeared in heaven: a woman clothed with the sun, with the moon under her feet and a crown of twelve stars on her head. She was pregnant and cried out in pain as she was about to give birth. Then another sign appeared in heaven: an enormous red dragon with seven heads and ten horns and seven crowns on its heads. Its tail swept a third of the stars out of the sky and flung them to earth. The dragon stood in front of the woman who was about to give birth, so that it might devour her child the moment he was born. She gave birth to a son, a male child, who "will rule all the nations with an iron scepter." And her child was snatched up to God and to his throne. The woman fled into the wilderness to a place prepared for her by God, where she might be taken care of for 1,260 days.*
>
> *Then war broke out in heaven. Michael and his angels fought against the dragon, and the dragon and his angels fought back. But he was not strong enough, and lost his place in heaven. The great dragon was hurled down—that ancient serpent called the devil, or Satan, who leads the whole world astray. He was hurled to earth, and his angels with him.*
>
> *Revelation 12:1–9 NIV*

That's a far cry from the Jesus in the manger story that we all know and love. Where is the manger? Where are the shepherds? A dragon? Sweeping its tail and wiping a third of the stars out of the sky? A war? Remember the heavenly host from the story in Luke? Here they are again, and this time they are at war! Consider what it says about Satan—"*who leads the whole world astray.*" More on that later.

Let's pick it up again in Revelation—

> *Therefore rejoice, you heavens and you who dwell in them. But woe to the earth and the sea, because the devil has gone down to you! He is filled with fury because he knows his time is short.*
>
> Revelation 12:12 NIV

So, the devil is here. On earth. And he is filled with fury.

> *Then the dragon was enraged at the woman and went off to wage war against her and the rest of her offspring—those who keep God's commands and hold fast their testimony about Jesus.*
>
> Revelation 12:17 NIV

This is also the story of the birth of Jesus. And, just as in the story from Luke Chapter 2, it is also all true. But it is from a different perspective. It is the story of the spiritual realm—the story of what was not seen. Satan has been flung from heaven to earth, along with one-third of the angels who are with him—his fallen angels or demons. He is filled with fury. And why is he filled with fury? Because he knows his time is short. That is important to remember. He knows it, and so should you. But he is waging war against us in the time he has left.

That friends, is spiritual warfare. And, just like the account from the Book of Revelation, it is mostly unseen in the physical world. And it is still happening. So that is why it is essential to be able to recognize it, even when you can't physically see it. Because if you don't recognize it, it can take you out.

I know that may sound frightening. But it doesn't have to be. God, in His unfailing, unconditional, and never-ending love for us, has given us everything we need to be prepared for these attacks and to resist them. To fight back. To conquer! God assures us in many ways that He is with us and will help us. We will review how He assures us to help and encourage us as we make our way through this book. But let's start with this—always remember the words of David in Psalm 23—

Even though I walk through the darkest valley,
I will fear no evil, for you are with me; your
rod and your staff, they comfort me.

Psalm 23:4 NIV

But before we go any deeper, I'd like to share a little about myself. I'm just an ordinary guy. I am married, with kids and grandkids. My wife and I face the same struggles that other couples face. I've spent most of my adult life in IT. I haven't attended seminary; I don't have a degree in theology. In fact, I don't have a degree in anything. So maybe you are thinking I'm not qualified to write a book on spiritual warfare. And if you are basing it on my background, then you are probably right. But as my wife will attest, I am spiritual, and I am persistent. (She calls it stubborn. Six of one, half a dozen of the other …) Once things started to be revealed to me, I wanted to know more. So, I dug in. I researched. I studied. I put it to the test. Maybe you think the same about yourself—that you're not qualified to *fight* a spiritual battle. We'll get into these thoughts as well. But let me assure you that if you are a follower of Christ, you are more than qualified. You are *Authorized*. You have been given authority. Although at this point, you may lack training. My prayer is that this book will help you in your preparation and that God will work through it to help you regain the full life that has been stolen from you.

CHAPTER 2

Recognizing Spiritual Warfare

God has given us everything we need to recognize, prepare for, resist, fight, and win the spiritual battles that will take place in our lives. And I do say battles, plural, because you will continue to face these battles until you die or until Jesus returns, whichever comes first. You have been under attack your entire life and may not even realize it, whether you are a follower of Christ or not. But as a follower of Christ, you have been given so much more to fight with, plus so much more additional protection! But before we get to that, let's spend some time looking at what I mean by attacks.

Scripture, which is one of our best weapons, warns us repeatedly about these attacks. In addition to what was just very clearly stated in Revelation, let's look at a few more verses:

… and do not give the devil a foothold.

Ephesians 4:27 NIV

Do not deprive each other except perhaps by mutual consent and for a time, so that you may devote yourselves to prayer. Then come together again so that Satan will not tempt you because of your lack of control.

> *1 Corinthians 7:5 NIV (Paul is addressing married couples specifically in this example)*

> *… in order that Satan might not outwit us. For we are not unaware of his schemes.*

> *2 Corinthians 2:11 NIV*

> *But I am afraid that just as Eve was deceived by the serpent's cunning, your minds may somehow be led astray from your sincere and pure devotion to Christ.*

> *2 Corinthians 11:3 NIV*

> *Then Peter said, 'Ananias, how is it that Satan has so filled your heart that you have lied to the Holy Spirit and have kept for yourself some of the money you received for the land?'*

> *Acts 5:3 NIV*

The warnings are there. It is evident that Scripture warns us about spiritual attacks.

Fruits of the Spirit Robbed

> *But the fruit of the Spirit is love, joy, peace, forbearance, kindness, goodness, faithfulness, gentleness, and self-control. Against such things there is no law.*

> *Galatians 5:22–23 NIV*

Take some time now. Stop and think. Pause here and meditate on this. Reflect on your life. Look deep into your heart. Is your heart filled with love? What about joy? Is there abundant joy in your life? Where are you looking for joy? Where are you looking for love? What about peace? Are you at peace with your life now? How about forbearance or patience and tolerance? Are you filled with kindness? How are you treating others? What about goodness? Faithfulness? Gentleness? Self-control? You get the point. All the Spiritual Fruits that Paul writes about in Galatians are meant to fill the hearts and lives of followers of Christ. Doesn't that sound wonderful? Doesn't it sound *full*? If you are feeling depleted in any of these areas, there is a good chance you are under spiritual attack. Jesus Himself said—

> *The thief comes only to steal and kill and destroy; I have come that they may have life, and have it to the full.*
>
> John 10:10 NIV

When we became followers of Christ, we were given the Holy Spirit. Paul tells us of the fruits that come from the Spirit, the fruits that come *with* the Spirit. Jesus tells us that we are meant to have life and have it to the *full*. Yes, we are guaranteed eternal life in Heaven through Jesus, but Jesus also said that we were meant to have life to the full, here and now, and that someone is trying to steal it!

I'll ask again—Is your heart filled with love? Are you feeling loved? Are you loving to others in your life? Or is your love being destroyed? What about joy? Is there abundant joy in your life? Is your joy being stolen? Is your kindness being killed? I know, I know, it is very easy to write things off—and yes, sometimes we all just have a bad day. Sometimes, we have a bad season. It's easy to tell yourself, "This isn't spiritual warfare; it's just a bad day." "This isn't spiritual warfare; this is just a bad situation that I'm going through right now." "This isn't the devil; this is just life, right?" Maybe. But maybe not. Jesus did say the thief comes only to steal, kill, and destroy.

Jesus also says this about the devil—

> *He was a murderer from the beginning, not holding to the truth, for there is no truth in him. When he lies, he speaks his native language, for he is a liar and the father of lies.*
>
> *John 8:44 NIV*

Do you think the devil wants you to know he is attacking you? Of course not! We'll get deeper into this in Chapter 9, but for now, understand—he lies. He deceives. And he wants to steal, kill, and destroy everything that Jesus wants you to have. Everything Jesus *died* for you to have. Yes, that's how much Jesus loves you. And that's how much the devil hates you.

> *You prepare a table before me in the presence of my enemies. You anoint my head with oil; my cup overflows.*
>
> *Psalm 23:5 NIV*

So, what might an attack look like in our lives? Rest assured, it's probably not the images portrayed in *The Exorcist*. It will likely be far more subtle. And it will likely be a slow depletion—a slow emptying. A drip here, a drip there, but soon, the once over-flowing cup is empty. Your heart will be emptied of the fullness that Christ intended for you.

Here's a recent example of one of my own personal attacks. When I felt the calling to write this book, I expected attacks. And sure enough, the attacks came. But, as mentioned, they were subtle. First, doubts entered my mind—"What are you doing? You can't write a book! You aren't an authority on this!" Then other, more disturbing thoughts of fear started to rise in me—"Why in the world would you actually study Satan? Why would you choose to learn about him? You are opening yourself up for attack! You will only make yourself vulnerable to him!"

Yes, there were doubts. Yes, there was fear. But I used what I have learned and will explain to you in this book to not only push through it but to rebuke it. To resist it, fight it, and conquer it. I know Satan does not want me to write this book as it may help others. He knows this and will use the power allowed to him to try to knock me off my feet. To prevent this book from being written and published. But, if you are reading or listening to this now, you will know his attacks were overcome.

You probably experience attacks that you attribute to everyday life. As I mentioned, it may seem as though it is just a bad day. Or just a tough time that you are going through. You may have thoughts of blame—blaming your situation on yourself or blaming your situation on others. I have also had these thoughts. Here is another recent example of mine. My mother has had some health issues lately. I have been staying with her to help care for her. My mother doesn't drive and relies on me to get her to her appointments, do her shopping, make sure she takes the right medicine dosage at the right time, prepare meals, do dishes, and do other small tasks. This current situation is temporary. I know this. But my mother lives 350 miles from my wife and me. I have been physically separated from my wife for over eight months now, and we have only been able to spend a total of five weeks together during this time. And the attacks come on both of us. We have both experienced doubt, *"This is not what marriage is supposed to be. This is not what I want in a marriage. This must not be meant to be."* For me, the attacks were worse. Much worse. There were doubts in myself. *"For this reason a man will leave his father and mother and be united to his wife, and the two will become one flesh" (Matthew 19:5 NIV).* And, of course, the marriage vows—*"What about forsaking all others—you are forsaking your wife! You are supposed to leave your mother and be with your wife!"*

Satan can and will try to confuse us, even with scriptures and things that seem good and right. For example, we know from the Gospels of Matthew, Mark, and Luke that Jesus was tempted by Satan in the wilderness. And in these temptations, Satan quotes Scripture to Jesus.

The Luke narrative states—

> *The devil led him to Jerusalem and had him stand on the highest point of the temple. "If you are the Son of God," he said, "throw yourself down from here. For it is written: 'He will command his angels concerning you to guard you carefully; they will lift you up in their hands, so that you will not strike your foot against a stone.'"*

> *Luke 4:9–11 NIV*

The devil knows Scripture. Here in Luke's Gospel, we see Satan himself quoting from Psalm 91:11. But remember, he is a liar—the father of all lies. We will dive deeper into understanding Satan in Chapter 9, but for now, understand that he may try to use and twist anything, including Scripture, against you, for he does know Scripture.

The Devil and the Angel

We've all seen the cartoon images of the little devil and the little angel sitting on someone's shoulders, whispering into their ear. The devil is red with horns and a little pitchfork. The angel is sweet, with wings and a tiny halo. And while this is a cartoon image, it is actually a good depiction of what happens to us each and every day. We all have thoughts of *"Should I, or shouldn't I?"* Guess what, friends? That is spiritual warfare. The devil and his demons are looking for ways to throw you off course. Again, spiritual warfare doesn't have to be graphic. Much more often, it is subtle. In the personal example I listed above, had I listened to the negative voice, this book would have been just a silly idea that I once had, placed on a shelf in the memories of my mind. And once placed there, it would have been much harder to bring it back into reality. Not impossible, for nothing is impossible with God, but much harder for me. Rather than rebuking the devil, I would have given him a foothold—a chance to firmly plant negativity.

The effects of this subtle spiritual warfare are cumulative. How many things have I given up on listening to fears and doubts? What wonderful things did God have in store for me that I missed out on just because I gave into fear and doubt?

Look at your own life. What things can you identify that you regret *not* doing? What riches may you have missed out on? This is yet again another type of spiritual attack—self-loathing. Once the devil talks you out of doing something good by leveraging fear and doubt or talks you into doing something wrong by leveraging selfishness and your feelings and emotions, he will then continue the attack, telling you that you were simply too weak. Too weak to do something good or too weak to resist something bad. He may also hit you with thoughts that you are simply a bad person, or God doesn't love you, or that you are in this all alone. It is a vicious cycle, friends. Remember, he is filled with fury. He is waging war against you.

> *Trust in the LORD with all your heart and lean not on your own understanding. In all your ways submit to him, and he will make your paths straight.*
>
> *Proverbs 3:5–6 NIV*

Here is a simple yet effective way to test the voices whispering in your ear. Does this voice whisper encouragement or discouragement? Pushing you to something wrong or pulling you into something righteous? Now, don't completely disregard discouragement. The Holy Spirit will also discourage you from doing wrong. But if what you are considering is something truly good and truly righteous, if it is something that will bear good fruit, you won't hear discouragement from the Holy Spirit. Instead, what you will hear is encouragement and guidance.

Let's look at some big events, just for clarity. Perhaps you are considering an affair. If a voice is encouraging that behavior, it is not of the Holy Spirit, as it directly conflicts with Scripture. Rest assured, that is a spiritual attack. The same holds true for divorce. Unless there has been sexual infidelity, Scripture condemns divorce. If sexual infidelity does not apply to your marriage, divorce conflicts with Scripture. Now, I am not encouraging anyone to stay in an abusive marriage by any means. Leave, and get yourself in a safe space. But even in cases of sexual infidelity or abuse, I believe any marriage can be healed and restored and can be a beautiful story of redemption, grace, mercy, compassion, and forgiveness that will bring Glory to God. Divorce will bring none of that. An affair will bring none of that. But what about these intense feelings that you may have? What if you feel like a divorce is the only way out? That you and your spouse weren't really meant to be together after all? Maybe it wasn't God's plan. You can't work through everything; there is just too much. If your feelings are pulling you away from scriptural truth, it's time to question them. It's time to put your feelings and understanding to the test of Scripture. Trust in God rather than your feelings. He is the creator of the universe. He is *your* creator, and you are created in His image.

> *Surely the arm of the LORD is not too short*
> *to save, nor his ear too dull to hear.*
>
> Isaiah 59:1 NIV

Healing a marriage takes trust and faith. Trust and faith in God, and trust and faith in your partner. Trust and faith in *yourself*. In many cases, it will take the help of others, perhaps a pastor, a Christian support group, a Christian counselor, or other believers that you can genuinely trust and confide in. Close friends that will give you sound scriptural and prayerful counsel.

> *Plans fail for lack of counsel, but with*
> *many advisers they succeed.*
>
> Proverbs 15:22 NIV

In every case, it will take prayer and submission to God.

Another quick test of the voices is this: Is this voice convicting you or condemning you? The Holy Spirit will bring conviction on you of things that you have done wrong, things you are doing wrong. This is out of love. He wants you to stop destructive behavior. Behavior that erodes your union with God. He wants to correct you and put you back on the right path. Condemnation is different—it tells you that you are no good. It tells you, "You are worthless." It tells you, "God doesn't love you" or "God has deserted you—you are on your own." See the difference?

Another way to recognize spiritual attack is that you may not recognize it as a spiritual attack. I know, I know, that sounds like a contradiction, but hear me out. It may not be apparent, and as I mentioned earlier, it will likely be more subtle than obvious. Since Satan is the father of all lies and a deceiver, it only makes sense that he will also lie to you and attempt to deceive you about his involvement in the attack itself. In his book *Wild at Heart*, author John Eldredge talks about the devil wanting to conceal himself. Eldredge recalls a conversation with a friend in which the friend shared with him about a staff meeting that had recently taken place at his church. The staff members were discussing some recent challenges, and the friend suggested that these challenges might be the work of the enemy. His idea was quickly dismissed. This is a church staff meeting! These are pastors, and the pastors themselves promptly dismiss the possibility of spiritual attack! John Eldredge sums it up this way—

> *"Nothing dangerous is happening here." Those men have already been taken out because they've swallowed the Enemy's first line of attack: "I'm not here – this is all just you." You can't fight a battle you don't think exists.*
>
> *John Eldredge—Wild at Heart: Discovering the Secret of a Man's Soul*[3]

---

[3] John Eldredge, *Wild at Heart Expanded Edition: Discovering the Secret of a Man's Soul*, Thomas Nelson, 2021.

Christian author C.S. Lewis highlights this same concept of the devil concealing himself in his book *The Screwtape Letters*, in which a senior-level demon is coaching his inexperienced protégé and gives the following advice:

> *Our policy, for the moment, is to conceal ourselves.*
>
> C.S. Lewis—*The Screwtape Letters*[4]

Understand that the battle is very real. The enemy is very real. He is a liar. He will attempt to deceive you in every possible way. And his first deceit will almost always be that it's not him.

Over the course of the next several chapters, we will examine the methods we can use to prepare ourselves for the battles we face.

---

[4] C.S. Lewis, *The Screwtape Letters: Annotated Edition*, ed. Paul McCusker, Harper Collins, 2013.

CHAPTER 3

Preparing Yourself for the Fight
Union With God

The LORD Is a Warrior, the LORD Is His Name.

*The LORD is my strength and my defense;
He is my God, and I will praise him. My
father's God, and I will exalt him. The LORD
is a warrior, the LORD is his name.*

Exodus 15:2–3 NIV

One of the first and most important things in your preparation is to not be afraid. As I mentioned earlier, this all sounds very frightening. But fear will always hold you back. In fact, fear is a very effective weapon in the devil's arsenal! To overcome this fear, it is of the utmost importance to understand, know, and believe that *God is with you* in this.

Let's look at the context around this verse from Exodus. Moses was called by God to lead the Israelites out of bondage in Egypt. God displayed many signs and wonders in Egypt, and finally, Pharoah agreed to release Moses and the Israelites. So the Israelites set out, off to the land God had promised their forefather Abraham some 400 years earlier.

But soon after their release, Pharoah had a change of heart. Scripture tells us that God hardened his heart—gave him even more resolve. Pharoah pursued the Israelites to capture them and bring them back to Egypt. Pharoah's chariots caught up to the Israelites as they camped at the edge of the Red Sea. The Egyptians were upon them, and they were trapped, with no place to go. Or so they thought. The angel of God, who had been traveling in front of the Israelites, now went behind them and stood between the Israelites and the Egyptian army as a pillar of cloud. Then God instructed Moses to raise his staff and stretch out his hand over the sea. God drove back the sea with a strong wind, and the waters of the Red Sea were divided. The Israelites went through the sea on a path of dry ground that God had made for them. The Egyptians pursued the Israelites, but God threw them into confusion and jammed their chariot wheels. The Egyptians realized this, but it was too late. After Moses and the Israelites had reached the other side of the Red Sea, Moses once again was instructed by God to stretch out his hand over the sea. In doing so, all the waters flowed back into place, drowning all the pursuing Egyptians. Moses and the Israelites then sang a song of praise to God—*"The LORD is a warrior; the LORD is his name."*

We are not in this fight alone! God can and will fight with us. He will fight for us! It is actually Him who fights our spiritual battles for us and through us—we just have to understand our authority in this and understand how to invoke it.

Knowing that God can and will fight with us—*fight for us*—is a tremendous comfort! And that is the first step. Knowing and believing that God will fight for us.

This and the following six chapters will cover preparing yourself. This is where most of the hard work will take place. Think about an athlete—they may take months or even years to train for and prepare for an event that may last only minutes. This is your training. *The LORD is a warrior; the LORD is his name.* And you, friends, were created in *His* image.

Union With God

> *I am the vine; you are the branches. If you remain in me and I in you, you will bear much fruit; apart from me you can do nothing.*
>
> *John 15:5 NIV*

Union with God is vital to every part of our lives as Christians. It was why we were created. We were created in God's own image. Our union with God is of the utmost importance when dealing with spiritual attacks. As Jesus says in John 15:5—*"apart from me you can do nothing."* Using the athletic training analogy I used earlier—What if God was your coach? What if God was calling each and every play? Having union with God will strengthen your faith. Reading and meditating on Scripture every day will help prepare you for the battles to come.

> *Let love and faithfulness never leave you; bind them around your neck, write them on the tablet of your heart.*
>
> *Proverbs 3:3 NIV*

> *These commandments that I give you today are to be on your hearts.*
>
> *Deuteronomy 6:6 NIV*

> *Fix these words of mine in your hearts and minds; tie them as symbols on your hands and bind them on your foreheads.*
>
> Deuteronomy 11:18 NIV

> *This is the covenant I will establish with the people of Israel after that time, declares the Lord. I will put my laws in their minds and write them on their hearts.*
>
> Hebrews 8:10 NIV

Make time every day to spend reading and meditating on God's word. If you say you just don't have time, I challenge you to look at your schedule. Are you ranking everything in your life of greater importance than spending time with God? Take some time to really think about the things that are keeping you busy. The things that you are giving priority. Are you making something an idol? Change your perspective. Make spending time with God a priority.

There are several methods for reading and journaling through the Bible. I like a method called SOAP, which is an acronym for Scripture, Observation, Application, and Prayer. Read your passage for the day, and see which verses stand out to you—that is Scripture. Ask the Holy Spirit to guide you in why the particular verses are speaking to you and ask Him to reveal them to you—that is Observation. Ask the Holy Spirit to guide you in how those particular verses apply to your life—that is Application. Ask God to help you use this Scripture the way He intended in your life—that is Prayer. My wife likes a method called the 4 Rs, which is similar—Read, Reflect, Respond, and Rest in God's Word. There are many methods, but all you really need to do is pray and ask God to speak to you, then just read!

> *Do not worship any other god, for the LORD,
> whose name is Jealous, is a jealous God.*
>
> Exodus 34:14 NIV

Putting other things ahead of God is giving them priority over God in your life. You may not be physically bowing down to them, but you are giving them priority over God, nonetheless.

Don't just carve out some time. It's really about realigning your life. If you try to squeeze a little of God into your life, well, you'll get a little of God. Build your life around God, and then align everything else with Him! Spending time with God is the best investment you can make! For some, mornings work best. For others, maybe in the quiet of the evening as they wind down their day. Personally, I like both. I like to start my day with prayer, then a Bible reading with a cup of coffee, then about 10 minutes of meditation. I also say prayers throughout the day. Not necessarily long, drawn-out prayers. In fact, some are just a few words. I also like prayer and meditation right before bed. Does it sound like a lot? Maybe it is to some people. For me, it is necessary. I *need* it. My union with God gets battered throughout the day, every day. Work stress, kids, family, shopping, the news, social media, you name it. It wears me down. From John 15:5, *"I am the vine; you are the branches."* I often see in my mind the image of a branch being torn from a vine. It is still hanging on, but there is some separation. Daily prayer and meditation graft my life, the branch, back into Jesus, the vine. I need to be restored in Christ daily. I need to be refreshed.

> *He refreshes my soul. He guides me along
> the right paths for his name's sake.*
>
> Psalm 23:3 NIV

It's not just the stresses of everyday life that can hinder our union with God. It can also be the choices we make. We talked earlier about sin. We will cover it more in the next chapter. Choosing to sin will also hinder our union with God.

> *See, I am setting before you today a blessing and a curse—the blessing if you obey the commands of the LORD your God that I am giving you today; the curse if you disobey the command of the LORD your God and turn from the way that I command you today ...*
>
> Deuteronomy 11:26–28 NIV

Moses is addressing the Israelites. He tells them clearly that they have choices, and with those choices come consequences—either blessings or curses.

> *Anyone who loves me will obey my teaching.
> My Father will love them, and we will come
> to them and make our home with them.
> Anyone who does not love me will not obey
> my teaching. These words you hear are not my
> own; they belong to the Father who sent me.*
>
> John 14:23–24 NIV

Note that here Jesus told the disciples that He and the Father will make their home with anyone who loves Him and obeys His teaching. Jesus is talking about union! Jesus wants to make His home with you, to dwell in you. But when you look away from Him and choose sin, you are turning your back on Him and running to something else. He is still there, knocking once again, ready to forgive over and over and over. Daily prayer and meditation are my way of turning back to Jesus every day.

> *All Scripture is God-breathed and is useful for teaching, rebuking, correcting and training in righteousness, so that the servant of God may be thoroughly equipped for every good work.*
>
> *2 Timothy 3:16–17 NIV*

A prayer for Union with God may look something like this:

> *Heavenly Father, Lord Jesus, Holy Spirit—I praise You for who You are. God Almighty—the creator of Heaven and earth, and my creator. You are my creator, and You created me in Your image. Thank You, God, for Your never-ending and unconditional love for me. Jesus, I come to You now to be restored in You and renewed in You. I come for refuge in You. Jesus, I get so battered every day from so many things in life. I give all these things to You now, Jesus. I give You everyone and everything. I give You all worry and anxiety. (Name the things here that have you worried and anxious. Be as specific as you can.) Holy Spirit, I ask You now to restore my union with the Father. Make me one with the Father, as Jesus is one with the Father. Restore my union with Jesus. Jesus, You are the vine. I am the branch. Remain in me, and restore me that I may remain in You. I want to bear fruit for You, Jesus. Apart from You, I can do nothing. Bring Your Kingdom and Your Will here on earth through me, Jesus. Restore me to do Your will.*

Thank You, Jesus. I love You, I trust You. I worship You. I ask this in Your name Jesus.

Amen.

Listening to God

> *For the word of God is alive and active*
>
> Hebrews 4:12 NIV

> *Blessed is the one who does not walk in step with the wicked or stand in the way that sinners take or sit in the company of mockers, but whose delight is in the law of the LORD, and who meditates on his law day and night. That person is like a tree planted by streams of water, which yields its fruit in season and whose leaf does not wither—whatever they do prospers.*
>
> Psalm 1:1-3 NIV

One of the most common ways God speaks to us is through Scripture. It draws us into Him and creates union with Him when we allow Him to speak to us.

I mentioned earlier that I spend time every day reading the Bible. There are so many great Bible-reading plans out there! I personally use the YouVersion Bible app[5] from Life. Church on my phone. At the time of this writing, the app has 69 English language translations of the Bible and well over 100 translations in other languages. YouVersion also has thousands of devotional and study plans that you can go through; many are only 4–5 days to complete, with a lot of

---

[5] YouVersion Bible App. Life.Church. Copyright 2008-2019.

different topics to choose from. Included in these plans are several "read the Bible in a year" plans. I go through the Bible every year using one of these plans. In going through the Bible from year to year, different things jump out at me each time. It's as if it was my first time ever reading it. The Word of God *is alive and active*. God will speak to you very personally through Scripture. I also find it helpful to pray before I start reading each day and ask God to speak to me. I ask Him to open my eyes to see, my ears to hear, my heart to receive, and my will to accept. Journaling can also be a great way to meditate on Scripture. Which verse or verses spoke to you? Why? Who did you relate with? Write it down. Go back through your journal from time to time. It's a great way to see how God is working in your life.

Another great resource I use daily is the *One Minute Pause*[6] mobile app from John Eldredge at *Wild at Heart/Ransomed Heart Ministries*. There are versions for both iPhone and Android available in the app store. There are several short meditations included that I find very helpful, and a fantastic 30-day meditation plan called *30 Days to Resilient*. It will take you through a 30-day journey of building true resilience through union with God, with short meditations each morning and evening. I highly recommend this as part of your walk with Jesus.

Whatever you choose must be right for you. But make sure it is rooted in Scripture, and make sure you spend time in Scripture every day. Make time for God *every* day to strengthen your union with Him.

---

[6] One Minute Pause, Ransomed Heart Ministries, Copyright Wild at Heart.

Listening for God

> *The LORD said, "Go out and stand on the mountain in the presence of the LORD, for the LORD is about to pass by." Then a great and powerful wind tore the mountains apart and shattered the rocks before the LORD, but the LORD was not in the wind. After the wind there was an earthquake, but the LORD was not in the earthquake. After the earthquake came a fire, but the LORD was not in the fire. And after the fire came a gentle whisper."*
>
> *1 Kings 19:11–12 NIV*
>
> *Be still, and know that I am God.*
>
> *Psalm 46:10 NIV*

God doesn't only speak to us through Scripture. Sometimes God will speak to us through other people. Have you ever attended a church service that felt like God was talking directly to *you*? He was. Ever heard a song or watched a movie that moved you in a way that you just can't describe? What about a sunset? Or a sunrise? The stars in the sky? Clouds? What about the sunlight reflecting on water? Thunder and lightning?

> *Holy, holy, holy is the LORD Almighty;*
> *the whole earth is full of his glory.*
>
> *Isaiah 6:3 NIV*

The earth is full of His glory. Since the earth is full of His glory, it certainly goes to reason that we can experience God and hear God through His glorious creation.

As I was beginning my time in prayer one morning recently, I was looking out the window. We just had a cold front move through, and the day was sunny, cool, and breezy. A beautiful and glorious day. As I was watching the breeze moving the branches on the trees, my focus jumped to one single leaf. I was drawn to this leaf. I was intrigued by this leaf. This one particular leaf, out of the thousands of leaves that were in my view, moving in the wind, caught my attention. It was moving much more rapidly than all the other leaves! I watched it for several minutes, marveling at its movement and wondering why it was moving so much more than the others. A verse came to mind:

*Wearing a linen ephod, David was dancing
before the LORD with all his might.*

2 Samuel 6:14 NIV

That's exactly what this single little leaf was doing! Dancing before the LORD with all its might! God brought that verse to me today through the Holy Spirit because of what I was experiencing of His glorious creation.

I have been driving lately with no music. It has become some of my best times with God. I often go for drives in the evenings. Recently, I drove out to some desert mountains west of here. It's dark and quiet. It had been a rough day. I started praying, and from out of nowhere, tears started coming. I asked God to reveal to me what I needed to do, what I needed to change. Here is what He said:

Be still, and know that I am God.

Psalm 46:10 NIV

I then left the mountains and drove to the church I used to attend about 15 years ago. It was there that I started learning more about the Bible, where I got my desire to learn more. When I was driving through the parking lot, I heard, *"I am the author and perfector of your faith."* I stopped to reflect on just how far God has taken me in the last several years. How much He has grown me. On my drive that night, God revealed that He is working in me. And it is a process that has taken years to get where I am. And I am thankful for everything and give all praise, glory, and honor to Him. Thank you, God!

On another night recently, I again went up into the desert mountains west of here. I started praying. It had been another rough day, and I felt very alone. I acknowledged in my prayer that I knew God was always with me, but I just wasn't feeling Him. I asked Him to please speak with me. I drove up to a little spot that I like. This particular spot up on the mountain overlooks the valley below. I parked, turned off my Jeep with the windows down in the dark, and was just still. In the cool of the desert evening, as I took in nature all around me and the twinkling lights of the city below, I felt a gentle breeze on my arm. I knew at that moment it was God showing me that He was with me. He told me to get out of the Jeep and look up. As I gazed upward, I saw the moon and all the stars shining in the night sky.

Lift up your eyes and look to the heavens: Who created all these? He who brings out the starry host one by one and calls forth each of them by name. Because of his great power and mighty strength, not one of them is missing.

Isaiah 40:26 NIV

God really came to me that night and showed me He is always right there with me.

In the fall of last year, while I was driving back from a client meeting, my wife sent me a text: *You have armed me with strength for the battle; you have subdued my enemies under my feet. 2 Samuel 22:40.* In addition to the verse, the text also included this prayer—"Dear Lord, Thank you in advance for removing the obstacles in my path. Guide my every step. I am following your lead." Along with a simple text that said, "I read this nice prayer today and thought you may like it too." What a blessing that prayer was to me that morning!

I would like to share with you another incredible story of God speaking. I was recently talking with my friend Jason. Jason is a firefighter and has been for more than 20 years. He has seen the worst of the worst in his service as a first responder. And, like so many others, the horrors he has witnessed over the years have taken their toll. His wife recently left him, and they are in the process of divorce. They have a young son, who is staying with Jason's wife. Jason has some land on which he is currently building a house. He was out there earlier this year, all alone. Alone in his thoughts. Feeling isolated. He began to make agreements with the lies being told to him by the evil one—"Everyone would be better off without you. Everyone's life would be better if you weren't here …" Jason grabbed a 12-gauge shotgun.

He has responded to many suicide calls over the years. He knows that a 12-gauge will end his life with certainty. The gun is loaded. The butt is on the ground, and Jason is looking down the barrel, reaching down with his hand, his finger resting on the trigger. Suddenly, he hears a voice commanding him—"*Stop!*" Jason is alone there. He puts down the gun and looks around. Not seeing anyone, he then walks around, looking for whoever spoke to him. He doesn't see anyone, but he knows who spoke to him. He thought he was alone. Very alone. But he wasn't.

Jason went to his superiors at work and told them what had happened. Suicide takes many, many more first responders than does dying in the line of duty. Agencies are becoming aware of this, and, luckily, Jason found inpatient help at a program designed specifically for first responders. His work is very supportive. He is doing well and returning to work soon to serve his community once again.

This is just one story. There are so many others that hear the voice of God in the critical moment and *listen* to Him! Unfortunately, there are many more that either don't hear or don't listen. But Jason *did* hear God that day, and I am so very thankful that he listened.

Several weeks passed after I saw the dancing little leaf. But it came back to me during my prayer and meditation time on another morning. I was once again looking out the window. My little leaf was not dancing on this particular morning. The leaf is on an orange tree. It was now late November, and the oranges were ripening. The branches were weighed down with heaviness. On this morning, *I was weighed down with heaviness.* "What is this heaviness, God?" I asked. As I started to write this question in my journal, the Holy Spirit started to reveal things to me before I had finished writing the question. There is no wind. There is no breeze. There is no *music*. Nothing to dance to.

In the fall of 2022, I was fortunate to attend a Wild at Heart Bootcamp in Colorado. It is a gathering of men from all across the country, the world, really. There were about 450 men in attendance from 46 states and 21 countries. It was really an amazing conference, but the reason I bring it up is this: I drove to Colorado from the Phoenix area to attend. Many people asked why I didn't fly. I could have flown in a couple of hours. It's a 13-hour drive from Phoenix. But I knew the drive would take me through northern Arizona, eastern Utah, and across northwestern Colorado. It would be beautiful scenery, and my heart *needed* it. I took pictures as I drove and sent them to my wife, along with messages like "My gosh, I can feel my heart coming alive! I can scarcely keep my eyes on the road from all the beauty that surrounds me." Re-reading that now, it sounds kind of poetic. Coming from an IT background for the last 30+ years, I have a tendency to be very analytical—working from the brain, not from the heart. It has been a point of frustration at times for my wife. But this drive! All the analysis just faded into the background of all the beauty spread out before me. The drive didn't tire me out; just the opposite. It refreshed me. Seeing God's glorious creation restored something in my heart.

    Back to this particular morning. I couldn't drive to Colorado again. It wasn't necessarily music that I needed but worship. I needed to be refreshed and restored in Jesus. In his book *Get Your Life Back*,[7] John Eldredge introduces the concept of Benevolent Detachment. Giving everything to God. Everyone and everything. Through the consistent practice of daily prayer and meditation, I meet Jesus in a particular place in my heart every day. It is on the beach in Coronado, CA, where my wife and I were married. It is only a few blocks from our home. My wife is usually with us when Jesus and I meet there. But many times, while I see Jesus standing in front of me, I can see His body, but I can't see His face. Honestly, I have struggled with giving things to Jesus. Fully letting go. My

---

[7] John Eldredge, *Get Your Life Back*, Thomas Nelson, 2020.

wife, our marriage, our kids, grandkids, my mother and her health, work, writing this book, finances, the list goes on and on. As I struggle to release these things, the Spirit takes me back to the words of Jesus in the Gospel of Luke—

Remember Lot's wife! Whoever tries to keep their life will lose it, and whoever loses their life will preserve it.

Luke 17:32-33 NIV

It really comes down to control. I need to trust in Jesus, that His ways are better than my ways. His love is better than my love. Release control.

Give all your worries and cares to God, for he cares about you.

1 Peter 5:7 NLT

Framed in this way, I can release those that I love and the things that I care about. I release my wife, our marriage, our kids and grandkids, my mother and her health, work, everything. I give everything back to Jesus. After all, it all belongs to Him anyway. He has only allowed me to steward over these people and things for a time. None of them, or any work, or any material thing, actually belong to me. They are His. I release them back to Him. One by one, I see my wife, our kids, grandkids, my mother, my laptop, and even my online banking app all go behind Jesus. Then, I see His face. He is smiling. I feel at peace. I feel a warming in my heart.

It can't all be about the battle, friends. We need to take the time to be refreshed and restored in Jesus. To come back into union with Him. We can't fight in our own strength. We can't just always try to push through in our own strength. We must have the strength of Jesus in everything, and we only receive it when we release everything to Him and take the time we need with Him in order to be refreshed and restored. We must surrender everything, including control, to Him.

As I continued in prayer and meditation, I again looked out the window. I'm looking back at the orange tree, just reflecting. In my peripheral vision, I see movement. My eyes are now fixed on another tree. There is a slight breeze blowing. Then I see it—a dancing leaf.

The LORD is a Warrior; the LORD is His name. The LORD is also love and beauty. The LORD is compassion, forgiveness, and mercy.

> *The LORD is gracious and compassionate,*
> *slow to anger and rich in love.*
>
> Psalms 145:8 NIV

> *If we confess our sins, he is faithful and*
> *just and will forgive us our sins and*
> *purify us from all unrighteousness.*
>
> 1 John 1:9 NIV

> *But because of his great love for us, God, who*
> *is rich in mercy, made us alive with Christ*
> *even when we were dead in transgression—*
> *it is by grace you have been saved.*
>
> Ephesians 2:4–5 NIV

My wife reminds me often of the need for balance. How she knows the needs of my heart! How true it is that we need balance. It can't always be about the fight. Your heart is more than just the fight. Allow yourself to fully experience all that God has for you—His glory and beauty and love all around us. The compassion and forgiveness that God has given to us through His grace and that we need to extend to others. Take the time to restore your union with God—all parts of God and all parts of you, every day. Your heart will thank you for it.

God will speak to you in many different ways. Sometimes, you just need to be still. And listen for Him.

He says, "Be still, and know that I am God; I will be exalted among the nations, I will be exalted in the earth."

Psalm 46:10 NIV

My sheep listen to my voice; I know them, and they follow me.

John 10:27 NIV

And if you are praying for God to speak to you, to reveal something to you, and you are not hearing Him, go back to Scripture. Search for the answer to your question in Scripture. He wants union with you—He wants you to know His word and wants to write in on your heart. Scripture is always our source of truth. It is God's truth and not the so-called truth of the world. Remember, our physical bodies are in the world. The world will always attempt to lead us into its false truths.

I am the way and the truth and the life.

John 14:6 NIV

Seek and you will find.

Matthew 7:7 NIV

A prayer for hearing God may look something like this:

Heavenly Father, Lord Jesus, Holy Spirit—I praise You for who You are. God Almighty—the creator of Heaven and earth, and my creator. You are my creator, and You created me in Your image. Thank you, God, for Your never-ending and unconditional love for me. Holy Spirit, Spirit of God, I ask You now to give me ears to hear. God, I need to hear You in my life. I need Your counsel. I need Your guidance. I need You, God. Holy Spirit, please let me know what I need to release to hear Jesus. Jesus, I want to hear Your voice. I need to hear Your voice. Father, forgive me for all the barriers I have put up, all the lies I have made agreements with that have kept me from hearing You. I ask now that You reveal these things to me so that I can truly repent of them. I want to have a deep and personal relationship with You, Jesus. I need union with You, Jesus. I want Your guidance. I need Your guidance. I need to hear Your voice, Jesus. Please speak to me through Your Word, through prayer, through the people You put in my life, and through creation. Jesus, You are my shepherd. I need to hear Your voice. I want to follow You. I choose to follow You, Jesus. Please give me the discernment to hear and know Your voice above all the noise, confusion, and chaos today, Jesus. Thank You, Jesus. I love You. I trust You. I worship You. I ask this in Your name Jesus.

Amen.

We live in a fallen world, friends. A world at war. But we also live in a world filled with God's glorious beauty! Seeking union with God every day will position you to see the beauty amidst the chaos and to hear Him speak to you.

The next chapter will require deep, authentic, and honest self-reflection. Take a breath, and let's get started.

CHAPTER 4

Preparing Yourself for the Fight
Sin, Repentance, Forgiveness, and Mercy

What is sin?

In Chapter 2, we looked at Galatians 5:22–23—the Fruits of the Spirit. In his letter to the church in Galatia, Paul wrote about the Acts of the Flesh and then contrasted it with the Fruit of the Spirit immediately after. What does Paul say about the Acts of the Flesh?

> *The acts of the flesh are obvious: sexual immorality, impurity and debauchery; idolatry and witchcraft; hatred, discord, jealousy, fits of rage, selfish ambition, dissension, factions and envy, drunkenness, orgies, and the like. As I did before, I warn you that those who live like this will not inherit the kingdom of God.*
>
> *Galatians 5:19–21 NIV*

I found many resources that give the history of the word sin as an archery term, in both Greek and Hebrew, that means "missing the mark."

Daniel Doriani, author and professor of theology at Covenant Seminary, defines sin in this way:

> *The Biblical Terminology of Sin. The vast terminology, within its biblical contexts, suggests that sin has three aspects: disobedience to or breach of law, violation of relationships with people, and rebellion against God, which is the most basic concept ... The Bible typically describes sin negatively. It is lawless ness, dis obedience, im piety, un belief, dis trust, darkness as opposed to light, a falling away as opposed to standing firm, weakness not strength. It is un righteousness, faithless ness.*[8]

The Bible describes it this way:

> *Everyone who sins breaks the law;*
> *in fact, sin is lawlessness.*
>
> 1 John 3:4 NIV
>
> *If anyone, then, knows the good they ought to do and doesn't do it, it is sin for them.*
>
> James 4:17 NIV

Sin erodes your union with God. It means you have turned your back to Him and chosen something else over Him. Chosen your way over His. It means you have attempted to elevate yourself over Him. But it does not mean you have separated yourself from His love. He is always right there, waiting for you, but He will let you make your choice. My friend and author Trent Renner explains it like this—"*God loves us so much that He will honor our choices. He will never*

---

[8] Daniel Doriani – www.biblestudytools.com/dictionary/sin

force Himself on us." You can find more of Trent's great teachings at www.trentrenner.com and www.returnhope.com.

Confessing Your Sins

We all sin. There is no denying it. That's the whole reason Jesus had to come, right? Confessing our sins and genuinely repenting will position us for the next steps.

> *If we claim to be without sin, we deceive ourselves and the truth is not in us. If we confess our sins, he is faithful and just and will forgive us our sins and purify us from all unrighteousness.*
>
> 1 John 1:8–9 NIV
>
> *We all, like sheep, have gone astray, each of us has turned to our own way.*
>
> Isaiah 53:6 NIV

So, who do we confess our sins to? Well, it may depend on the sin, but the first place to always start is to confess your sin to God. Some sins in your life may be evident to you. It may be something you have struggled with for years—pride, arrogance, anger, lying, or idolatry. For some, it may be an addiction. Some sins may be evident and known to others. Others may be hidden deeply away. For some struggles, seeking professional Christian counseling may be the right step. Don't let pride or shame stop you from seeking help. There is no more shame in counseling than going to a doctor or dentist.

And to make you aware, idolatry does not have to be bowing down and worshipping a stone or wooden carving. An image of Buddha. One of the many Hindu gods. No, idols can be much more subtle than that. Anything you put ahead of your relationship with God Almighty is an idol. Do you spend more time balancing your checkbook and checking your stock portfolio than you spend with God? Do you get so wrapped up in work that you aren't taking a few minutes throughout the day to check in with God? Are you putting your relationships with friends, family, and even your kids and spouse ahead of your relationship with God? There are many, many things that we can easily allow to become idols in our lives without even realizing it.

Included among such idols, there may also be other sins that aren't evident to you. Pray about them. David, a great warrior himself, prayed this:

Search me God, and know my heart; test me and know my anxious thoughts. See if there is any offensive way in me, and lead me in the way everlasting.

Psalm 139:23–24 NIV

Confession of some sins may require you to trust in others and perhaps to ask to be held accountable.

Therefore confess your sins to each other and pray for each other so that you may be healed. The prayer of a righteous person is powerful and effective.

James 5:16 NIV

If your sins have caused pain to others, you will need to confess to them as well. Jesus gives two very practical examples of this—

Therefore, if you are offering your gift at the altar and there remember that your brother or sister

> *has something against you, leave your gift there in front of the altar. First go and be reconciled with them; then come and offer your gift. Settle matters quickly with your adversary who is taking you to court. Do it while you are still together on the way, or your adversary may hand you over to the judge, and the judge may hand you over to the officer, and you may be thrown into prison.*
>
> *Matthew 5:23–25 NIV*

In the first example, you know something you have done wrong. You confess your sin to the person you have wronged. In the second example, perhaps you were unaware of your offense, but it has been brought to your attention. In both instances, Jesus teaches us to quickly make things right with the other person. Prolonged unresolved conflict invites spiritual warfare.

> *In your anger do not sin: Do not let the sun go down while you are still angry, and do not give the devil a foothold.*
>
> *Ephesians 4:26–27 NIV*

Note that Paul says, "In your anger do not sin." Being angry in and of itself is not a sin. Paul was talking specifically about anger here. Anger is an emotion, just as happiness is an emotion. But it's what you do or don't do with your anger or other emotions that matter. There are accounts in the Bible of Jesus becoming angry. One of the most well-known accounts is Jesus clearing the temple courts:

> *When it was almost time for the Jewish Passover, Jesus went up to Jerusalem. In the temple courts he*

> *found people selling cattle, sheep and doves, and others sitting at tables exchanging money. So he made a whip out of cords, and drove all from the temple courts, both sheep and cattle; he scattered the coins of the money changers and overturned their tables. To those who sold doves he said, "Get these out of here! Stop turning my Father's house into a market!" His disciples remembered that it is written: "Zeal for your house will consume me."*
>
> *John 2:13–17 NIV*

Was Jesus angry? Heck yes, He was angry! People were attempting to profit by selling sacrifices for those that came to worship at the temple for the Passover. Did Jesus sin in His anger? No, but He certainly got His point across. He also didn't sit on His anger. He didn't let the sun go down on His anger.

Confession is a crucial step in preparing yourself. If we attempt to engage the devil and his demons with unforgiven sin in our lives, our attempts will not be effective. But we are promised that by confessing our sins, we will be forgiven.

> *If we confess our sins, he is faithful and just and will forgive us our sins and purify us from all unrighteousness.*
>
> *1 John 1:9 NIV*

A prayer for confessing your sins to God may look something like this:

Heavenly Father, Lord Jesus, Holy Spirit—I praise You for who You are—God Almighty—the creator of Heaven and earth, and my creator. You are my creator, and You created me in Your image. Thank You, God, for Your never-ending and unconditional love for me. Thank You for proving Your love for me by sending Jesus as a sacrifice. Jesus, thank You for giving Your life for me. No one took it from You, but You gave it willingly and lovingly. Jesus, I honor You as my Lord. Thank You, Jesus.

Jesus, I confess to you now my sin of (Tell Jesus about your sin. There is no shame here. Don't hold back—He already knows your sin. He wants to hear you tell Him about it, not to shame you, but to heal you.) Jesus, I am truly sorry; I ask Your forgiveness for this sin. Your word tells us that if we confess our sins to You, we will be forgiven. Jesus, thank You for this merciful promise. I believe You that I will be forgiven. That I am forgiven. Jesus, search my heart and reveal to me other areas where I have sinned. Jesus, I ask You to come into the wounds in my heart that this sin has caused. Please meet me there and heal me. Thank You, Jesus. I give You all glory, honor, thanks, and praise. I love You, Jesus. Jesus, I ask this in Your name.

Amen.

When you confess your sins to others, pray beforehand. If the other person is willing, praying together with that person as you begin your conversation would be beneficial. That prayer may look something like this:

Heavenly Father, Lord Jesus, Holy Spirit—I (or we) praise You for who You are. God Almighty—the creator of Heaven and earth, and my (our) creator. You are my (or our) creator, and You created me (or us) in

Your image. Thank You, God, for Your never-ending and unconditional love for me (or us). Jesus, I (or we) ask in Your name now that You would send the Holy Spirit to fill my heart and to fill the heart of (name the person that you will be confessing to). Jesus, I (or we) ask that Your Holy Spirit lead this conversation in loving truth. Jesus, I (or we) ask that You would be with us both, come into the wounded places in our hearts, heal us individually, and heal and restore the damage to the relationship that this sin has caused. Jesus, we ask this in Your name.

Amen.

Things may get emotional. Anger may come. Tears may come. But complete healing will never come without confessing. So take the time to pray through it—again together, if possible. And if the person won't hear you out, or won't speak to you, or maybe this person is no longer living, you can still get complete healing by confessing this to Jesus.

Repentance

After you confess your sins, there must be repentance. What exactly is repentance? Google defines repentance as "The action of repenting; sincere regret or remorse."[9]

The key phrase there is *sincere regret or remorse*. I'm sure we've all heard, and perhaps participated in ourselves, an almost bragging kind of confession: "I partied sooo hard last night!" That may be a confession, but that is *not* repentance. True repentance includes regret and remorse. Wikipedia goes

---

[9] Google's English Dictionary is provided by Oxford Languages.

further: "Repentance is reviewing one's actions and feeling contrition or regret for past wrongs, which is accompanied by a commitment to and actual actions that show and prove a change for the better."[10]

King David puts it beautifully—

> *My sacrifice, O God, is a broken spirit; a broken and contrite heart you, God, will not despise.*
>
> *Psalm 51:17 NIV*

I've often heard the word repent described as turning away from something.

This is the true repentance that is required of us. We must feel true remorse for the things we have done wrong *and* show true commitment to change, as well as actions that prove change. This goes back to our confessions of sins to those we have hurt. Our confession must also show remorse, and our repentance will show through our actions that we truly are changing and turning away from those behaviors and turning to God. An apology of "I'm sorry that you felt hurt by what I did" is not remorseful. When we apologize in that way, we aren't apologizing for what we have done; we are only saying we are sorry that they felt that way. That puts the wrong back on them, as though they are wrong for feeling hurt. It does not show remorse or repentance on our part. We need to apologize for our actions, which brought about their hurt, and show true change. Don't let pride get in the way of repentance. Life is too short. Make your amends. Tomorrow is not guaranteed.

As a side note here—you may have been the recipient of the "I'm sorry you feel that way" type of apology. My

---

[10] En.wikipedia.org/wiki/Repentance

suggestion, friends, is to show grace, accept, and forgive. Even if the genuine apology that shows remorse never comes, you must forgive.

We all sin, and we are all called to repent. So instead of holding on to self-loathing and regret about your sin, look at repentance as an opportunity to learn and grow. It is healing, my friends.

> *Repent, then, and turn to God, so that your sins may be wiped out, that times of refreshing may come from the Lord.*
>
> Acts 3:19 NIV

> *Produce fruit in keeping with repentance.*
>
> Matthew 3:8 NIV

> *This is what the Sovereign LORD, the Holy One of Israel, says: "In repentance and rest is your salvation."*
>
> Isaiah 30:15 NIV

A prayer for repentance may look something like this:

Heavenly Father, Lord Jesus, Holy Spirit—I praise You for who You are. God Almighty—the creator of Heaven and earth, and my creator. You are my creator, and You created me in Your image. Thank You, God, for Your never-ending and unconditional love for me. Jesus, I come to You now to ask for Your mercy, grace, and deliverance from this (name the sin) that has held me captive. Jesus, I want You as the center of my life—I need You as the center of my life. Grant to me now Your deliverance from this (name the sin), and grant to me a true repentance. Fill me with Your Holy Spirit, and lead me on the right path, Your path, the path that leads to life. I choose You, Jesus, over this (name the sin). Through Your never-ending love and wisdom, give me the discernment to know the lies, schemes, and deceit of the evil one. Give me Your strength and power to resist and rebuke him at all times. Jesus, I ask this in Your name.

Amen.

Forgiveness

This brings us to the other side of confession, apology, and repentance. Forgiveness. Don't hold on to unforgiveness. Even if the person who has wronged you never confesses or apologizes, you must forgive.

I have heard it said that there are three sides to every story—my side, your side, and what really happened. We all see things through our own lens. We create our own account of what happened from our own viewpoint and perspective. My wife has been so good at helping me to see things from someone else's perspective. She has this gift. She is an empath. For me, it is something that I must continually work on. But it is something that I am trying to cultivate in my own heart. To open my heart to see others and understand them. But we don't have to understand to forgive. Understanding will help us to heal relationships that have been damaged. Some things we may never understand. But we can't hold onto unforgiveness.

"Unforgiveness is like drinking poison and expecting someone else to die." This quote has been attributed to several different people, but the message is clear: If you hold on to unforgiveness, it will ultimately harm you. Forgiving someone does not say that the hurt you experienced wasn't real or that it was ok. It is simply letting it go. Another popular saying, attributed to many different people, is this: "Don't let someone live rent-free in your head." Unforgiveness takes so much more time and energy from your emotions and spirit than just simply releasing it—giving it to Jesus and being free of it. I know it can be easier said than done. But with practice, you can do it. You just have to start. And if you have to release the same thing over and over again, do it. Jesus tells us of the severe ramifications of not forgiving others:

For if you forgive other people when they sin against you, your Heavenly Father will also forgive you. But if you do not forgive others their sins, your Father will not forgive your sins.

Matthew 6:14–15 NIV

Wow. That's pretty weighty. Let's let that sink in—if we don't forgive others, we won't be forgiven. Again, in what is commonly known as The Lord's Prayer, Jesus says:

And forgive us our debts, as we also have forgiven our debtors.

Matthew 6:12 NIV

Forgive us our debts, as we have also forgiven our debtors. Jesus is not giving us this as an option. It is laid out as a condition.

Again, Jesus teaches us about forgiveness:

Then Peter came to Jesus and asked, "Lord, how many times shall I forgive my brother or sister who sins against me? Up to seven times?" Jesus answered, "I tell you, not seven times, but seventy-seven times."

Matthew 18:21–22 NIV

Meaning seventy *times* seven times. And no, Peter, that still is not a hard limit! Have you sinned more than seventy times seven times in your life? Of course, you have! And does God have a hard limit on how many times He will forgive us? Thankfully, no! And that is wonderful news for us! The point Jesus is making here is that we should never stop forgiving. We are called to love. Remember the Fruits of the Spirit? Love, Joy, Peace, Forbearance, Kindness, Goodness, Faithfulness, Gentleness, and Self-control. None of those seems to line up with unforgiveness and resentment. In fact, it will be difficult to bear any kind of spiritual fruit if you are holding on to unforgiveness and resentment in your heart. Unforgiveness actually seems to fit nicely into impurity, hatred, discord, selfish ambition, and dissension, all described by Paul as acts of the flesh, as we discussed earlier in this chapter. Are you having trouble forgiving? Ask Jesus about it! Ask Him for help. Ask Him to meet you in these places in your heart. Ask Him for healing. It may take time. It may take lots of prayer. It may take repetition. And that's ok! Jesus loves it when we pray to Him. He wants that deep relationship. He wants to have that deep relationship with you! He is waiting for you—

Here I am! I stand at the door and knock. If anyone hears my voice and opens the door, I will come in and eat with that person, and they with me.

Revelation 3:20 NIV

What does Jesus mean when He says, "I will come in and eat with that person, and they with me"? Here's a clue:

> Then Jesus declared, "I am the bread of life. Whoever comes to me will never go hungry, and whoever believes in me will never be thirsty."
>
> John 6:35 NIV

> You prepare a table for me in the presence of my enemies. You anoint my head with oil; my cup overflows.
>
> Psalm 23:5 NIV

Letting Jesus into all those places of unforgiveness and resentment can be so fulfilling, so rewarding, so healing, and so freeing. He is there. He is knocking. He wants to prepare a table for you. He wants to feed you. Yes, right in the middle of everything that you are going through. Will you let Him in?

And please. Please. Please forgive yourself. God has forgiven you.

> If we confess our sins, he is faithful and just and will forgive us our sins and purify us from all unrighteousness.
>
> 1 John 1:9 NIV

Friends, holding unforgiveness in your heart is a place you are withholding from Jesus. This includes unforgiveness for yourself. As for me? I'm my own worst critic. But over time, I've come to realize that it's not really me that is unwilling to forgive myself. Rather, it is agreements that I have made with the evil one when he puts those ideas in my head. "Oh, that thing I did was sooo, sooo bad. Wow—I really am a horrible person. I am really screwed up. I am an evil person. I am not worthy of God's love. I am not worthy of God's gifts and blessings." Friends, if you have confessed, you have been forgiven! These things in your head are lies from the evil one, and you must rebuke them. Don't make agreements with them! And if you have made agreements with them, you must renounce them. God has forgiven you. You must forgive yourself.

> *Godly sorrow brings repentance that leads to salvation and leaves no regret, but worldly sorrow brings death.*
>
> *2 Corinthians 7:10 NIV*

A prayer for forgiveness may look something like this:

Heavenly Father, Lord Jesus, Holy Spirit—I praise You for who You are. God Almighty—the creator of Heaven and earth, and my creator. You are my creator, and You created me in Your image. Thank You, God, for Your never-ending and unconditional love for me. Jesus, I ask You now to fill me with Your Holy Spirit. Fill my mind with life and peace; fill my heart with love. Jesus, come into my heart now in the wounded place of (name the wound that you have and who wounded you). Jesus, this wound hurt me. It mattered. But I don't want to hold this resentment and unforgiveness in my heart, God. I forgive (name the person) for (name the wound). I fully and completely forgive them. Jesus, I invite You now into this wounded place in my heart. Please meet me here and heal and restore this wound in my heart, Jesus. I give You this wound now, Jesus. I fully and completely release it to You. Jesus, I ask in Your name that complete forgiveness of (name the person) and full healing take place now. Thank You, Jesus.

Amen.

Sometimes, if wounds are deep or this has been unforgiven for a long time, the devil may have a stronghold here. He may have been attacking you again and again in this wound for a very long time. He does not want you to forgive because then he loses his foothold. You may have to revisit this and forgive several times. Do it again and again if you still feel unforgiveness. But you must forgive. When you hold this in your heart, it is a place that you have closed off to Jesus, and Jesus wants your whole heart. Again, forgiveness does not excuse what was done to you. It doesn't mean that it didn't hurt you or that it didn't matter. It only means that you are now releasing it, so it no longer has power over you.

Mercy

The next step after forgiveness is mercy. Think of mercy as pre-meditated forgiveness, especially when you have the power or authority to punish someone in some way for an offensive action. It is acceptance of people's imperfections and humanity. As followers of Christ, we have been extended mercy from God. We, in turn, are called to extend mercy to others.

As I have mentioned, my wife has helped me tremendously with this. Seeing things from another person's perspective, or *through their lens,* as she calls it. I see her practicing this with other people. She practices this with me as well, but sometimes in my stubbornness, it can be difficult for me to see it. But she has such patience with me, and I am thankful for it. Others throughout my life have helped me in this way as well—teaching me great lessons in mercy by extending mercy to me.

My dad taught me a valuable lesson in mercy very early in my life. My dad passed away in 2014. We were luckier than so many others. My dad didn't have a long, drawn-out illness. He had been in the hospital for about two weeks, admitted with abdominal pain, which turned out to be an infection. We weren't too worried at first. Things seemed to be going well. In fact, he was released after a few days, not to go home, but to a facility for some rehab. But then, he took a turn for the worse and returned to the hospital, this time to the ICU. There were some good days filled with hope, but during his last week, my days were mostly filled with the reality of what was happening—my dad was dying.

I remember the doctor having a hard conversation with us. They wanted to intubate him. The previous days had been filled with a delicate balancing act—fighting infection and trying to avoid fluid buildup in his lungs. Constantly monitoring his condition and changing meds as needed. We had plenty of those conversations with the doctor, but this conversation was different. We understood that this was really the last resort. It was a Monday. My dad showed some improvement on Tuesday but took a turn for the worse on Tuesday night. On Wednesday morning, they let us know that it was a losing battle.

My dad had always said he never wanted to be kept alive by a machine. And machines were all that were keeping him alive by this point. We had some time to say our goodbyes. The machines were turned off. Our pastor was in the room with us. My dad passed very peacefully on a Wednesday late in the afternoon.

My family came to the Southwest from the Midwest. We have lots of extended family back there. My mom and dad, years before this, had purchased burial plots in Missouri, in their hometown. My mom and I wrapped up as many loose ends as we could on our end, then headed back to Missouri. We made arrangements with the funeral home, church, and cemetery.

So what does this have to do with mercy? Two days prior to the funeral, my mom asked me if I would write and deliver the eulogy. She had very good reasoning. We had lived away from Missouri for many years. This minister really didn't even know my dad. I told my mom that I would, but I really had no idea what to say or how to say it. I prayed that God would give me the right words.

The night my dad passed, I posted about it on Facebook. I received lots of condolences and support, for which I am thankful. But one comment, in particular, stood out to me. It was from my friend and previous pastor, Trent Renner. His comment said, "What a great man. He will be missed, and followers of Christ will see him again someday. Head up, Mike, your dad is now in what Hebrews 12:1 calls the cloud of witnesses. Larry is sitting in the Grandstands of Heaven. May our lives be of such, as we fill the big shoes of your dad, that we make Larry stand and cheer for joy as he watches us! Mike, you will see your dad again, but not yet! Love ya, man."

Trent was and still is the best Bible teacher that I have ever had. He taught us to put things in context. If we didn't have the context, read a few more verses. Read the previous verses. Read the whole chapter, but get the context. So ... what exactly is the cloud of witnesses? I read all of Hebrews 12. Then, I went back to Hebrews 11. Hebrews 11 reads like a Who's Who heroes of the Bible. Able, Enoch, Noah, Abraham,

Sarah, Jacob, Joseph, Moses, the list goes on. And it talks about their faith. So when Hebrews Chapter 12 starts, it says:

> *Therefore, since we are surrounded by such a great cloud of witnesses, let us throw off everything that hinders us and the sin that so easily entangles. And let us run with perseverance the race marked out for us.*
>
> *Hebrews 12:1 NIV*

So, the great cloud of witnesses is? Everyone that has passed before us and gone to Heaven. They *witness* us! They *surround* us! This is also clear biblical evidence that there is an unseen spiritual world that surrounds us. Hebrews 12 goes on to say:

> *And have you completely forgotten this word of encouragement that addresses you as a father addresses his son? It says, "My son, do not make light of the Lord's discipline, and do not lose heart when he rebukes you, because the Lord disciplines the one he loves, and he chastens everyone he accepts as his son." ... For what children are not disciplined by their father?*
>
> *Hebrews 12:5–7 NIV*

A memory sparked, and I knew God had given me my dad's eulogy. A story about his mercy.

When I was about five years old, a friend and I went around the corner to watch the big kids. You know, the 10–12-year-olds. They had taken a cinder block and an old 2x10 and made a ramp. They were jumping their bikes, and it was so cool for a 5-year-old to watch! The problem was my mom had no idea where I was.

Now, as kids, we spent nearly all day outside. But it was usually out in the yard or on the street in front of the house. My mom could look out the window and see us. But now, my friends and I were no place to be found. For nearly an hour. My mom called everyone else's mom, but no one knew where I was. My mom was worried. She got in the car to start looking. And when she came around the corner, there we were, cheering as the big kids launched their bikes into the air. Her worry quickly turned to anger—"Why didn't you tell me where you were? Do you know how worried I have been? You are going to deal with your father!" Wait, what? Nooo! Not dad! I was about to get a beating for sure. Not that I had ever had a beating, but I was sure I was in for one.

My mom dragged me into the house. I was pleading for her to punish me instead of my dad. She handed me to him and went into the other room. My dad looked down at me. He didn't say a word. He sat on the couch and laid me over his lap. Here it comes! I was bracing for the pain I knew my backside was about to experience. He laid his big left hand over my butt, then strongly smacked the back of his own left hand with his right. The smack was LOUD! Several more smacks followed. My backside remained intact, but I'm sure my dad's left hand was glowing red. He then picked me up, gave me a quick wink, and told me to go to my room to think about what I had done. My mom heard the smacks, thinking that I had gotten quite the spanking. My dad, having been a boy once himself, understood what I had done. He also understood why my mom was so worried. He did discipline me that day, but he also taught me a valuable lesson about mercy and a father's love for his son.

I shared this story at my dad's funeral. I talked about the cloud of witnesses and that I knew my dad was still watching over me. I still feel many of his lessons in my life today, including mercy.

> *This is what the LORD Almighty said:*
> *"Administer true justice; show mercy*
> *and compassion to one another."*
>
> *Zechariah 7:9 NIV*

What happens when we don't show mercy? Let's look again at what Jesus has to say about forgiveness, continuing with mercy.

> *Then Peter came to Jesus and asked, "Lord, how many times shall I forgive my brother or sister who sins against me? Up to seven times?"*
>
> *Jesus answered, "I tell you, not seven, but seventy-seven times."*

Therefore, the kingdom of heaven is like a king who wanted to settle accounts with his servants. As he began the settlement, a man who owed him ten thousand bags of gold was brought to him. Since he was not able to pay, the master ordered that he and his wife and his children and all that he had be sold to repay the debt.

At this the servant fell on his knees before him. "Be patient with me," he begged, "and I will pay back everything." The servant's master took pity on him, canceled the debt and let him go.

But when that servant went out, he found one of his fellow servants who owed him a hundred silver coins. He grabbed him and began to choke him. "Pay me back what you owe me!" he demanded.

His fellow servant fell to his knees and begged him, "Please be patient with me, and I will pay it back."

But he refused. Instead, he went off and had the man thrown into prison until he could pay the debt. When the other servants saw what had happened, they were outraged and went and told their master everything that had happened.

Then the master called the servant in. "You wicked servant," he said, "I canceled all that debt of yours because you begged me to. Shouldn't you have had mercy on your fellow servant just as I had on you?" In anger his master handed him over to the jailers to be tortured, until he should pay back all he owed.

This is how my heavenly Father will treat each of you unless you forgive your brother or sister from your heart.

Matthew 18:21–35 NIV

My friends, God has shown each and every one of us His great mercy.

But you, O Lord, are a God merciful and gracious, slow to anger and abounding in steadfast love and faithfulness.

Psalm 86:15 ESV

Righteousness and justice are the foundation of Your throne; Mercy and truth go before You.

Psalm 89:14 NASB2020

> *The LORD is gracious and merciful, slow to anger and abounding in steadfast love. The LORD is good to all, and his mercy is over all that he has made.*
>
> Psalm 145:8–9 ESV

> *The steadfast love of the LORD never ceases; his mercies never come to an end; they are new every morning; great is your faithfulness.*
>
> Lamentations 3:22–23 ESV

God's mercies never come to an end; they are new every morning. Friends, let's strive to be the same. Mercy and forgiveness, given by God, lead to mercy and forgiveness given by us. It is good for our souls.

> *The merciful man does good for his own soul, But he who is cruel troubles his own flesh.*
>
> Proverbs 11:17 NKJV

We have looked deep inside ourselves at our sinful nature, how we can repent, and how we need to forgive and show others mercy, just as we have been forgiven and shown mercy. This chapter may have made you uncomfortable with some areas of your life—and that's not a bad thing! Remember, this is training, and training can be hard. Is fear getting in the way? Is pride getting in the way? We've all heard the phrase "no pain, no gain." Push through the pain, and don't give up! Ask Jesus for His help and His strength to get you through this. Trust in Him.

In the next chapter, we will look at how faith, trust, and the Holy Spirit all work together to help us in these battles.

CHAPTER 5

Preparing Yourself for the Fight
Faith, Trust, and the Holy Spirit

Faith

> *But blessed is the one who trusts in the LORD, whose confidence is in him. They will be like a tree planted by the water that sends out its roots by the stream. It does not fear when heat comes; its leaves are always green. It has no worries in a year of drought and never fails to bear fruit.*
>
> *Jeremiah 17:7-8 NIV*
>
> *Now faith is the confidence in what we hope for and the assurance about what we do not see.*
>
> *Hebrews 11:1 NIV*

Faith and trust go hand in hand. They are complementary. Our trust grows as our faith grows.

When my girls were small, probably from about the age of one through six or seven, we had this little game we would play. Actually, more of an activity. We called it up-downs. I would pick up one of my daughters, and holding them under their arms, I would throw them up into the air, then catch them as they came back down. They loved it!

They would ask me to do it over and over until my arms were too tired to continue. The first time they tried it, they were scared! They had a panicked look in their eyes. But as soon as they came down and I caught them, their fear turned to joy. They wanted to do it again and again; it was their hope. It was fun. It was exhilarating. For them and for me! I loved hearing their laughter. I can still hear it today. They are memories that I cherish.

As I mentioned, the first time any of my girls tried it, they were afraid. But then, when they saw that I had caught them, they trusted me. Of course, there was already a level of trust before we tried it for the first time. That was faith—they knew from past actions that I had no intention of letting them get hurt. As trust grows, so does faith. Hope then grows from faith. Hope is looking forward. Faith is belief in what you have seen or experienced, what you have grown to trust. Our trust, faith, and hope in God are the same as the trust, faith, and hope that my daughters had in me at such a young age. I use this as a simplistic example. My daughters, however, at such a young age, hadn't experienced many of the pains, heartaches, and letdowns that life brings to all of us. Don't let your life experiences with other people shape your trust, faith, and hope in God. People, even the ones you love the most, even the ones who love you the most, can and will let you down in so many ways.

Another odd example of faith and trust that I can share is with my fat little one-eyed chihuahua named Luna. Ok—no body shaming here—Luna isn't fat. She's voluptuous! Luna is a rescue. And I didn't pick her—she picked me. On a Saturday several years ago, the local pet store had an adoption event. I wasn't looking for a dog that day. I had gone to the store adjacent to the pet store, and the adoption event caught my eye. I walked over and was looking at the dogs that were up for adoption. Some were running around playing with one another in their little pens, and others were sitting quietly toward the back of the enclosure. Luna was one of the latter. But when I walked up, she immediately ran to the front of the pen, got up on her back legs, tail wagging, just begging to be petted and loved. I reached down and gave her a good scratch behind the ears, then a little scratch under her chin. She licked my hand, then I moved down the line. As soon as I left her, she went back to reclaim her position at the back of the pen. I walked down to the end of the line, then turned and made my way back. As I approached her enclosure again, she raced back up to the front, up on her back legs again, tail wagging. The rest, as they say, is history. Luna came home with me that day. She had picked me.

I've had many dogs over the years. From small chihuahuas to a Neapolitan Mastiff. I've loved them all, but none have been quite like Luna. She trusts me like no other dog I have ever had. She loves to be cradled in my arms like a baby, literally on her back, completely vulnerable, just waiting for love and belly rubs. She trusts me. She knows I won't drop her. She knows I won't harm her. She is completely surrendered to me as she is cradled there in my arm. And you know what? I love giving her those belly rubs! I love holding her. As a rescue, I don't know her background. I don't know how she lost her eye. I do know that she picked me. Ran to me. Trusted me. I've often asked myself, how different could my life be if I trusted God as much as this little dog trusts me? Had faith in Him as much as she has faith in me? Surrendered to Him as much as little Luna surrenders to me? Let God love me the way she lets me love her? Oh, how God longs for us to completely surrender to Him! And He has so much more to offer us than belly rubs!

> *I have come that they may have*
> *life, and have it to the full.*
>
> John 10:10 NIV

As I mentioned earlier about not letting your mistrust of the world shape your trust in God, well, I sometimes fit squarely into that category. But as I also mentioned, trust grows faith, and faith grows hope.

And I, as I suspect you, friends, are, in so many ways, among good company in our struggles with faith and trust. Jesus hand-picked each of His disciples with the simple invitation— *"Follow me."* His disciples were a rag-tag group, to be sure. We know from Scripture that Andrew and his brother Simon (Peter) were fishermen, as were the brothers James and John. We know that Matthew was a tax collector, and tax collectors were despised among the Jews. We know the other Simon was a zealot, not a profession per se, but the zealots were anarchists bent on overthrowing the Roman government. We're not told the professions of the other Apostles, but I think we can rest assured this was a motley crew. And Jesus reminded them time and time again about their faith or lack thereof.

> *Then he got into the boat and his disciples followed him. Suddenly a furious storm came up on the lake, so that the waves swept over the boat. But Jesus was sleeping. The disciples went and woke him, saying, "Lord, save us! We're going to drown!" He replied, "You of little faith, why are you so afraid?" Then he got up and rebuked the winds and the waves, and it was completely calm.*
>
> Matthew 8:23–26

Six chapters later, Matthew describes another time the disciples were in a boat with Jesus.

> *Immediately Jesus made his disciples get into the boat and go on ahead of him to the other side, while he dismissed the crowd. After he had dismissed them, he went up on a mountainside by himself to pray. Later that night, he was there alone, and the boat was already a considerable distance from the land, buffeted by the waves because the wind was against it.*
>
> *Shortly before dawn Jesus went out to them, walking on the lake. When the disciples saw him walking on the lake, they were terrified. "It's a ghost," they said, and cried out in fear.*
>
> *But Jesus immediately said to them: "Take courage! It is I. Don't be afraid." "Lord, if it's you," Peter replied, "tell me to come to you on the water." "Come," he said. Then Peter got down out of the boat, walked on the water and came toward Jesus. But when he saw the wind, he was afraid and, beginning to sink, cried out, "Lord, save me!" Immediately Jesus reached out his hand and caught him. "You of little faith," he said, "why did you doubt?"*
>
> Matthew 14:22–31

Yes, even those hand-picked disciples that physically walked side by side with Jesus for three years, heard Him teach every day, and watched Him perform repeated miracles, still lacked faith. So please, friends, don't be too hard on yourselves as your faith grows. You are in good company. And let's tie hope into this now as well—

> *And run with endurance the race set out for us, keeping our eyes fixed on Jesus, the pioneer and perfecter of our faith.*
>
> Hebrews 12:1–2 NET

We are all a work in progress. While we go through life and our progress, we must trust in God and have faith and hope in the truth that Jesus is the start of our faith, and He will perfect our faith. Please understand that perfecting our faith is an ongoing process—a process that will continue until we die or until Jesus returns. We will continue to grow spiritually. When we understand that spiritual growth, which includes perfecting our faith, is a process, it helps us from becoming discouraged, which is what our enemy wants. This can be extremely difficult in the world we live in today. Our microwave society and our own mentality want and expect instant gratification. And while God can certainly provide instant deliverance at times, more often than not, He is using opportunities and situations we find ourselves in to grow us spiritually, including growing our faith.

And all believers do have faith! When we accepted Jesus as our Lord and Savior, we were given faith by God himself:

> *… in accordance with the faith God has distributed to each of you.*
>
> Romans 12:3 NIV

Jesus will grow your faith. Spending time with Him every day will increase it abundantly.

> *Consequently, faith comes from hearing the message, and the message is heard through the word about Christ.*
>
> Romans 10:17 NIV

Faith and the Fight

> *The apostles said to the Lord, "Increase our faith!" He replied, "If you have faith as small as a mustard seed, you can say to this mulberry tree, 'Be uprooted and planted in the sea,' and it will obey you."*
>
> Luke 17:5-6 NIV

So how does faith tie into everything?

Let's take a look at an account from the Gospel of Luke:

> *Now when Jesus returned, a crowd welcomed him, for they were all expecting him. Then a man named Jairus, a synagogue leader, came and fell at Jesus' feet, pleading with him to come to his house because his only daughter, a girl of about twelve, was dying. As Jesus was on his way, the crowds almost crushed him. And a woman was there who had been subject to bleeding for twelve years, but no one could heal her. She came up behind him and touched the edge of his cloak, and immediately the bleeding stopped. "Who touched me?" Jesus asked. When they all denied it, Peter said, "Master, the people are crowding you and pressing against you." But Jesus said, "Someone touched me; I know that power has gone out from me." Then the woman, seeing that she could not*

> *go unnoticed, came trembling and fell at his feet. In the presence of all the people, she told why she had touched him and how she had been instantly healed. Then he said to her, "Daughter, your faith has healed you. Go in peace." While Jesus was still speaking, someone came from the house of Jairus, the synagogue leader. "Your daughter is dead," he said. "Don't bother the teacher anymore." Hearing this, Jesus said to Jairus, "Don't be afraid; just believe, and she will be healed." When he arrived at the house of Jairus, he did not let anyone go in with him except Peter, John and James, and the child's father and mother. Meanwhile, all the people were wailing and mourning for her. "Stop wailing," Jesus said. "She is not dead but asleep." They laughed at him, knowing that she was dead. But he took her by the hand and said, "My child, get up!" Her spirit returned, and at once she stood up. Then Jesus told them to give her something to eat. Her parents were astonished, but he ordered them not to tell anyone what had happened.*
>
> Luke 8:40–56 NIV

What a beautiful account of faith and belief. This account is also told in the Gospel of Matthew and Mark. Let's look at another example:

> *Then they came to Jericho. As Jesus and his disciples, together with a large crowd, were leaving the city, a blind man, Bartimaeus (which means "son of Timaeus"), was sitting by the roadside begging. When he heard that it was Jesus of Nazareth, he began to shout, "Jesus, Son of David, have mercy on me!" Many rebuked him and told him to be quiet,*

> but he shouted all the more, "Son of David, have mercy on me!" Jesus stopped and said, "Call him." So they called to the blind man, "Cheer up! On your feet! He's calling you." Throwing his cloak aside, he jumped to his feet and came to Jesus. "What do you want me to do for you?" Jesus asked him. The blind man said, "Rabbi, I want to see." "Go," said Jesus, "your faith has healed you." Immediately he received his sight and followed Jesus along the road.
>
> *Mark 10:46–52 NIV*

Now let's look at a different example:

> When Jesus had finished these parables, he moved on from there. Coming to his hometown, he began teaching the people in their synagogue, and they were amazed. "Where did this man get this wisdom and these miraculous powers?" they asked. "Isn't this the carpenter's son? Isn't his mother's name Mary, and aren't his brothers James, Joseph, Simon, and Judas? Aren't all his sisters with us? Where then did this man get all these things?" And they took offense to him. But Jesus said to them, "A prophet is not without honor except in his own town and in his own home." And he did not do many miracles there because of their lack of faith.
>
> *Matthew 13:53–58 NIV*

Let's look at the same account from the Gospel of Mark:

> Jesus left there and went to his hometown, accompanied by his disciples. When the Sabbath came, he began to teach in the synagogue, and

many who heard him were amazed. "Where did this man get these things?" they asked. "What's this wisdom that has been given him? What are these remarkable miracles he is performing? Isn't this the carpenter? Isn't this Mary's son and the brother of James, Joseph, Judas, and Simon? Aren't his sisters here with us? And they took offense to him. Jesus said to them, "A prophet is not without honor except in his own town, among his relatives and in his own home. He could not do any miracles there, except lay his hands on a few sick people and heal them." He was amazed at their lack of faith.

Mark 6:1–6 NIV

Notice in this account Mark says Jesus *could not* do any miracles there. Now, I don't put any limits on the power of God whatsoever. But this does tell me how vital faith is on our part. If we don't have faith, we cannot expect Jesus to deliver us from the trials we are experiencing. It is our faith in Him, not ourselves that allows the Holy Spirit to work in us.

You may wonder how you can increase your faith. One great way to increase faith is by reading the Bible. Scripture will reveal to you that time and time again, God does come to the rescue! He does deliver His people from their troubles, and if you have faith, He will deliver you as well. It may not always be within your timeframe or in the way you expected. But He will deliver you if you have faith. Another way to increase your faith is to ask Jesus for help.

A prayer to increase faith may look something like this:

Heavenly Father, Lord Jesus, Holy Spirit—I praise You for who You are. God Almighty—the creator of Heaven and earth, and my creator. You are my creator, and You created me in Your image. Thank you, God, for Your never-ending and unconditional love for me. Jesus, I ask You now to fill me with Your Holy Spirit. Heal and restore faith in me, Jesus. Grow faith in me, Jesus; increase faith in me. I love You, I trust You, I believe You, Jesus. Restore faith in me, Jesus. Strengthen my faith, Jesus. You are the author and perfector of my faith, Jesus. Open my heart to receive faith from You, Jesus. I love You, Jesus, and I ask this in Your name.

Amen.

Trusting in God

> *Abram believed the LORD, and he credited it to him as righteousness.*
>
> *Genesis 15:6 NIV*

Before God gave him the name Abraham, he was named Abram. God told Abram that, even though Abram and his wife were childless and getting old, God would give them a son, their own flesh and blood. And in addition to that, his offspring would be greater than the number of stars in the sky that could be counted. Abram trusted God and believed Him. After Abraham's son Isaac was born, God tested Abraham and asked Abraham to sacrifice his son Isaac. Abraham again trusted God, and God stopped Abraham just before he sacrificed Isaac and provided a ram for the sacrifice.

> *By faith Abraham, when God tested him, offered Isaac as a sacrifice. He who had embraced the promises was about to sacrifice his one and only son, even though God had said to him, "It is through Isaac that your*

> *offspring will be reckoned." Abraham reasoned that God could even raise the dead, and so in a manner of speaking he did receive Isaac back from death.*
>
> Hebrews 11:17–19 NIV

Faith takes trust, and if you are anything like me, trust can be difficult. We have all been wronged by not only strangers and those we don't know but also by those that we know and love—co-workers, close friends, and even family. Even those closest to us—our parents, our children, and our spouses. These wrongs are often accompanied by hurt and pain. *"How could they do that to me?"* is the question we often ask ourselves. And trust is broken. But we know the whole world is broken. As we are seeing, the world is at war. There are casualties. And often, we are the casualties. It is easy to lose trust in others. And from our own wounds and experiences, it is easy to be wary. It is easy not to trust. It's an instinctive self-protection mechanism. It's fight or flight. We will discuss this more in Chapter 8 as well.

So how can we trust God? Maybe the first question is—why should we trust God?

> *For God so loved the world that he gave his one and only Son, that whoever believes in him shall not perish but have eternal life.*
>
> John 3:16 NIV

Yes, that is probably the most quoted verse from the Bible. Quoted so often that we may not really stop to consider exactly what is being said. For those of you with children, consider this: Would you sacrifice one of your children to save someone else? I've heard many stories of parents with such giving hearts that when one of their children dies, they let the organs be used to save another. This is such a beautiful and giving thing to do in their grief. And many say that their child would have wanted it that way. And that speaks greatly to the wonderful person their child was. But this isn't organ donation. This is sacrifice. God sacrificed Jesus so that we can be with Him for eternity. He doesn't want to lose us. That's how much He loves us. God loves you so much that He allowed Jesus, no, not just allowed—He *sent* Jesus to earth for the very purpose of being a sacrifice for us.

Why did there have to be a sacrifice anyway? The Bible is filled with examples of sacrifice as atonement for sin. There are many examples in Leviticus, but for this question, let's look at Exodus:

> *Tell the whole community of Israel that on the tenth day of this month each man is to take a lamb for his family, one for each household. If any household is too small for a whole lamb, they must share one with their nearest neighbor, having taken into account the number of people there are. You are to determine the amount of lamb needed in accordance with what each person will eat. The animals you choose must be year-old males without defect, and you may take them from the sheep or the goats. Take care of them until the fourteenth day of the month, when all the members of the community of Israel must slaughter them at twilight. Then they are to take some of the blood and put it on the sides and tops of the doorframes of the houses where they eat the lambs.*
>
> *On that same night I will pass through Egypt and strike down every firstborn of both people and*

> *animals, and I will bring judgment on all the gods of Egypt. I am the LORD. The blood will be a sign for you on the houses where you are, and when I see the blood, I will pass over you. No destructive plague will touch you when I strike Egypt.*
>
> *Exodus 12:3–7, and 12–13 NIV*

> *For the life of a creature is in the blood, and I have given it to you to make atonement for yourselves on the altar; it is the blood that makes atonement for one's life.*
>
> *Leviticus 17:11 NIV*

There was no other way. God determined the amount needed. God sacrificed His only Son because Jesus was the only sacrifice that could cover all the sins of humanity. Jesus is the ultimate sacrifice. He is the Son of God! Jesus is pure and without defect. His blood had to be shed, and His life had to be given.

So, back to the question of trust. Yes, it is easy to have mistrust. But can you allow yourself to trust the One that loves you so much that He sacrificed His only Son for you? That's how much God loves you. He has proven His love for us. That's how much we can trust Him. I know for me personally, in many regards, trust must be earned. Trust can be fully given only when someone has proven themselves trustworthy. God the Father has proven His love for us by sending Jesus. And Jesus gave His life for you—

> *"The reason my Father loves me is that I lay down my life—only to take it up again. No one takes it from me, but I lay it down of my own accord."*

John 10:17–18 NIV

Life was not taken from Jesus. He gave His life. Willingly and lovingly, He gave His life. For you. Jesus has proven Himself trustworthy.

When you hear the voice telling you something, or have that urge, or you are feeling led to do something, and it seems so real and so true, ask yourself—"Does this align with the Word of God? Does it align with Scripture?" Scripture should always be the authority. Always. It is trustworthy. That is why it is so important to spend time in Scripture every day. Knowing God's Word matters. It can, and it will save you.

Jesus calls the devil "the father of lies." And Paul tells us in 2 Corinthians, "Satan himself masquerades as an angel of light." Yes, the devil's lies can seem so, so true. But his ultimate goal is to kill, steal, and destroy, remember? God loves you so much that He sent Jesus to die for you so that He can spend eternity with you. Satan, on the other hand, hates you. He wants to steal eternity with God from you. He wants to separate you from God. He wants to steal from you the full life that God wants for you. That's how much Satan hates you. He is not trustworthy. And he has proven himself not to be trustworthy. He will lie, scheme, and deceive you however he can. Remember, he is waging war against you.

The devil is the father of lies, but God is the God of truth. The Word of God is truth. The best way to know the truth is to read it and study it. Friends, I can't urge you enough to spend time in Scripture every day.

*These commandments I give you
are to be on your hearts.*

Deuteronomy 6:6 NIV

> *Keep my commands and you will live; guard my
> teachings as the apple of your eye. Bind them on
> your fingers; write them on the tablet of your heart.*
>
> Proverbs 7:2–3 NIV

> *I will put my law in their minds and write it on their
> hearts. I will be their God, and they will be my people.*
>
> Jeremiah 31:33 NIV

God wants us to know His Word. He wants us to have His Word. He wants to write it on our hearts! I ask you now to take a little time. Memorize the following two verses:

> *Trust in the LORD with all your heart and lean
> not on your own understanding; in all your ways
> submit to him and he will make your paths straight.*
>
> Proverbs 3:5–6 NIV

> *There is a way that appears to be right,
> but in the end it leads to death.*
>
> Proverbs 16:25 NIV

When you feel you are being led in a certain direction, always make sure that it aligns with the written Word of God. Always make sure it aligns with Scripture. Always. Remember the image of the devil and the angel sitting on your shoulder? One will always lead you to God's truth. The other will always lead you away from God's truth. It will erode your union with God. Always. Friends, I can't stress this enough! Understand—our feelings and emotions are not a bad thing! God has given them to us! But the evil one will try to use our feelings and emotions to deceive us. If it sounds like I am over-emphasizing this, well, I am! It is that important! Always let Scripture be your authority. Yes, God does speak to us in other ways beyond Scripture. But the evil one speaks to us, too, and he will always try to deceive you. He comes to steal, kill, and destroy. We can't always trust our feelings or our emotions. The very free will that God gives us is the very thing that Satan will use to attack us the most.

A prayer to increase trust may look something like this:

Heavenly Father, Lord Jesus, Holy Spirit—I praise You for who You are. God Almighty—the creator of Heaven and earth, and my creator. You are my creator, and You created me in your image. Thank you, God, for Your never-ending and unconditional love for me. Jesus, I ask You now to fill me with Your Holy Spirit. Heal and restore my trust in You, Jesus. I love You, and I believe You, Jesus. Restore my trust in You, Jesus. Strengthen my trust in You, Jesus. Jesus, my heart has been hardened. My heart has been hardened by this broken world. Open my heart to trust You, Jesus. Jesus, You proved Your love for me by going to the cross lovingly and willingly. You have proven Yourself trustworthy, Jesus. I love You, Jesus, and I ask in Your name to restore my trust in You.

Amen.

Agreements

I was first introduced to spiritual agreements by the author John Eldredge. He sums up agreements this way:

> *We want to be as clear as possible what we mean by an "agreement."*

Satan is a liar, "the father of lies" (John 8:44), so utterly convincing he deceived a glorious man and woman to betray God, whom they walked with every day. I think we tend to dismiss Adam and Eve as the idiots who got us all into this mess in the first place. But they had not yet sinned; they had experienced no wounding; they were man and woman in their glory. And they were deceived. It ought to give us all a healthy respect for what the enemy is capable of.

Even the best of us can be taken in.

What Satan is hoping to secure from us is an agreement—that often very subtle but momentous shift in us where we believe the spin, we go with the feeling, we accept as reality the deception he is presenting. (It always feels so true). Just settle for what you've got. Don't risk being hurt again. Once we buy into the lie, make the agreement, we come under the spell, come under the influence of that interpretation of events. Then it pretty much plays itself out; it becomes self-fulfilling. These agreements begin to define the relationship. They certainly color the way we experience one another. It can be devastating to just let this stuff roll on unchecked and unchallenged. Look what happened to Adam and Eve.

The first thing we want to do is recognize what's happening as the enemy presents an agreement, and give it no quarter. Fight it, resist it, send it packing to the outer reaches of hell. Recognize what is at stake here.

> *The kingdom teeters on the hundred small choices we make every day.*
>
> *Now, many of these agreements are already deeply rooted in our lives, some of them so historic and familiar we barely even recognize them. So, how do we acknowledge them?*
>
> *Well (this will be an absolute epiphany) ask Jesus.*[11]
>
> *John and Stasi Eldredge – Love & War*

Note how John and Stasi say that many of these agreements are already rooted deeply in our lives. Let's go back to what Paul tells us in Ephesians—

> *In your anger do not sin: Do not let the sun go down while you are still angry, and do not give the devil a foothold.*
>
> *Ephesians 4:26–27 NIV*

Paul used the emotion of anger, but I believe any emotion when spun with the lie we believe, can give the devil a foothold. And when they are allowed to stay for a long time, they become deep-rooted. They become a stronghold. And, as John and Stasi say, the agreement becomes self-fulfilling.

Let's reflect on that for a minute. Self-fulfilling. Let's look back on the creation. God spoke the entire universe into creation. God said, *"Let there be ..."* and it happened. Then God created humans. But He didn't speak us into creation.

---

[11] John and Staci Eldredge, *Love and War: Find Your Way to Something Beautiful in Your Marriage*, Waterbrook, 2011.

> *Then God said, "Let us create mankind in our image, in our likeness …"*
>
> Genesis 1:26 NIV

Genesis 2 goes into a little more detail:

> *Then the LORD God formed a man from the dust of the ground and breathed into his nostrils the breath of life, and the man became a living being.*
>
> Genesis 2:7 NIV

> *So the LORD God caused the man to go into a deep sleep; and while he was sleeping, he took one of the man's ribs and then closed up the place with flesh. Then the LORD God made a woman from the rib he had taken out of the man, and he brought her to the man.*
>
> Genesis 2:21–22 NIV

God didn't simply speak us into creation as He did everything else. He formed us. Made us. This was much more intimate. And He created us in His image. We know that God's words have power. He did speak the entire universe into creation! And, since God made us in His image, I believe that our words also have power. Scripture does not disagree with this.

> *The tongue has the power of life and death, and those who love it will eat its fruit.*
>
> Proverbs 18:21 NIV

> *From the fruit of their lips people are filled with good things, and the work of their hands brings them reward.*
>
> Proverbs 12:14 NIV

> *The words of the reckless pierce like swords, but the tongue of the wise brings healing.*
>
> Proverbs 12:18 NIV

> *Likewise, the tongue is a small part of the body, but it makes great boasts. Consider what a great forest is set on fire by a small spark. The tongue is also a fire, a world of evil among the parts of the body. It corrupts the whole body, sets the whole course of one's life on fire, and is itself set on fire by hell.*
>
> James 3:5–6 NIV

Our words have power, my friends. The power to build others up or to tear them down. But also the power to build ourselves up or tear ourselves down. Self-fulfilling. David knew the power our words have and asked God for help.

> *Set a guard over my mouth, LORD; keep watch over the door of my lips.*
>
> Psalm 141:4 NIV

With my friend Jason the firefighter, the agreement nearly became tragically self-fulfilling. Had he not listened to the voice that said "Stop!" the lie would have been fulfilled. The longer these agreements go on unchecked, and the more agreements that are made, after time, the devil's foothold becomes a stronghold.

I did touch on agreements in Chapters 3 and 4, but I felt that more of an explanation needed to be given. I went back and forth about whether to put this section in Chapter 4 but was led to put it in this chapter instead because the ability to break agreements really comes down to trusting Jesus. Again, because the lies can seem so real, it is important to listen to and trust God. And, in the case of lies and agreements, go back to Scripture. The written word of God, which is truth. Scripture will reveal the devil's lies.

And though we touched on it in Chapter 2, it's worth revisiting. Another clue to know whether the voice in your head may be the evil one—is it putting you down? Does it condemn you? Lies like "I'm not good enough," "I don't deserve this," or "I'm such a bad parent." Maybe it's not outright condemnation, but is it seeking to steal your joy or to steal a gift that God gave to you? "This marriage will never work," or "I'll never be able to heal the relationship with my brother," or "I will never be able to get along with these people at work," or "I just can't do this." If the voice is telling you something about yourself, and it includes *never* or *always*, that should always cause you to take notice and look for the lie. When looking at a spiritual attack, look at the *never* or *always* that is true— God will never leave you. God will never forsake you. God will always love you. God will always be there for you.

Since learning about agreements, I have unpacked and renounced many agreements that I have made. Some go all the way back to childhood. Agreements like "You are in this alone," "There is no one to help you," "You have to figure this out on your own," and "If you ask for help, you will be seen as weak." And, as John and Stasi said, ask Jesus! Talk to Him about your fears and doubts. Talk to Him about how you are being attacked. Ask the Holy Spirit to lead you. And always remember what Jesus said—

> *The thief comes only to steal and kill and destroy; I have come that they may have life, and have it to the full.*
>
> *John 10:10 NIV*

The devil wants to steal, kill, and destroy everything that God wishes to give you. He is waging war against us.

Two specific types of agreements I want to make you aware of are *I deserve* and *I don't deserve* agreements. Both can be very easy to agree with, and both can be very dangerous. And both of these types of agreements are fed to us daily, not only by ourselves but also by friends, family, and most all types of media. Let's look first at the *I deserve* agreements.

I deserve agreements are typically rooted in pride, but some *I don't deserve* agreements can be as well. They can feed our egos and are, in fact, mostly ego driven. "I've worked hard; I *deserve* a new car," or "*I deserve* a new house." "*I deserve* this vacation." "*I deserve* a raise," or "*I deserve* a better job." Now, friends, *"I need"* or *"I would like"* are not the same as *"I deserve."* In the examples above, a new car, a new house, or a vacation may very well be needed, and it is ok to want these things! Just don't fall into the *I deserve* agreement. These agreements can also make us look down on and judge others, "*I deserve* to be with someone better," or "*I don't deserve* to be treated like this by my friend." When you catch this, don't take the bait! Turn it into an *"I would like"* or *"I need"* statement instead.

The other *I don't deserve* types of agreements are those that are rooted in self-loathing, *"I don't deserve your love,"* or *"I don't deserve this nice of a gift."* Not only can they be rooted in guilt and self-loathing, but if someone is trying to give you something nice, just to be nice, with no strings attached, you could be robbing them of a blessing. If you are saying you don't deserve God's love or His blessings, well, that is a true statement. None of us deserve them, but by His grace and His love for us, He gives them anyway. So let Him! Accept them with thanks.

Look for the deeper meaning behind any agreement as well. What is happening in your life when Satan is trying to get you to make an agreement? What was happening in your life when you made an earlier agreement? What was God trying to give you? What was Satan trying to block? By breaking agreements, we can flip them around! We can be the victors God intended us to be and not the victims Satan is trying to make us. Pause and reflect on what God may be trying to teach us—perhaps patience or unconditional love. Perhaps mercy or forgiveness. How will God use what Satan is attempting to do as a way to grow us spiritually?

If you believe you have made agreements, again, it would also be very beneficial to use Scripture for the truth to contradict these agreements. Google is your friend here! Just make sure you are searching and looking only for Scripture verses applicable to your agreement. But don't go down the rathole of looking at countless opinions of others that you may find on what you are dealing with. As well-meaning and well-intended as they may be, at times, they could take you off course and actually strengthen the agreement. Stick to God's truth.

A prayer against agreements may look something like this:

Heavenly Father, Lord Jesus, Holy Spirit—I praise You for who You are. God Almighty—the creator of Heaven and earth, and my creator. You are my creator, and You created me in Your image. Thank you, God, for Your never-ending and unconditional love for me. Jesus, I ask You now to fill me with Your Holy Spirit. Jesus, forgive me for the agreement I made with (list your agreement here. An example is "I am alone with no one to help me." If you have multiples, ask for forgiveness for each of them.) In the name of the Lord Jesus Christ, I renounce the agreement I made with (name your agreement. If you found truth in Scripture that contradicts the lie, it is helpful to name it here—with the example of "I am alone with no one to help me," a useful Scripture would be "God has said 'I will never leave you; never will I forsake you'" Hebrews 13:5 NIV). The lies I believed and the agreements I made with (name the agreement) are now broken, canceled, and disarmed. Jesus, I know these agreements left me with wounds. Jesus, I ask You now to come into my heart. Meet me in the wound that this (name with agreement) has made. Heal and restore my heart Jesus; heal and restore my union with You. Father, Lord Jesus, Holy Spirit, search me, know me, and reveal to me any agreements I have made that I may not be aware of. (Pause and listen. If nothing else is revealed to you, continue.) I love You, Jesus, and it is in Your name I pray.

Amen.

More agreements may be revealed to you at a later time. Agreements are still being revealed to me. God is gentle. His healing is gentle. He may not reveal everything to you at once.

Has the Holy Spirit Become Diluted?

There are so many great examples in the Bible of the Holy Spirit working in and through God's people to accomplish great things. Here are some great examples from John Eldredge:

> *The Philistines went up and camped in Judah, spreading out near Lehi. The men of Judah asked, "Why have you come to fight us?" "We have come to take Samson prisoner," they answered, "to do to him as he did to us." Then three thousand men from Judah went down to the cave in the rock of Etam and said to Samson, "Don't you realize that the Philistines are rulers over us? What have you done to us?" He answered, "I merely did to them what they did to me." They said to him, "We've come to tie you up and hand you over to the Philistines." Samson said, "Swear to me that you won't kill me yourselves." "Agreed," they answered. "We will only tie you up and hand you over to them. We will not kill you." So they bound him with two new ropes and led him up from the rock. As he approached Lehi, the Philistines came toward him shouting. The Spirit of the LORD came upon him in power. The ropes on his arms became like charred flax, and the bindings dropped from his hands. Finding a fresh jawbone of a donkey, he grabbed it and struck down a thousand men. Then Samson said, "With a donkey's jawbone I have made donkeys of them. With a donkey's jawbone I have killed a thousand men."*
>
> *Judges 15:9–16 NIV*

A Sunday school story? Perhaps. Though I have never heard the lesson explained, "And this, children, is what happens when the Spirit of God comes upon a man." Yet that is clearly the lesson of the passage. Samson becomes a great and terrible warrior when, and only when, the Spirit of God comes upon him. The rest of the time he's just short of an idiot. What does this story tell us about the God who the Spirit is? And it's not just Samson, my friends. "So the Spirit of the LORD came upon Gideon," and Gideon went to war (Judges 6:34 NASB). "Now the Spirit of the LORD came upon Jephthah," and he went to war (Judges 11:29 NASB). "And the Spirit of the LORD came mightily upon David," and one of the first things he did was kill Goliath (1 Samuel 16:13 NASB). I repeat my question: What does that tell us about the God who the Spirit is?[12]

John Eldredge – All Things New

John leaves us with that question—What does that tell us about the God who the Spirit is? I believe it confirms what we reviewed earlier—

The LORD is a warrior, the LORD is his name.

Exodus 15:3 NIV

But we can't expect to fight evil spirits in our own power. We would get taken out in very short order. Up until this time, you may not have been fighting them at all. You may have just been chalking up attacks to circumstances, a bad day, or the

---

[12] John Eldredge, *All Things New: Heaven, Earth, and the Restoration of Everything You Love*, Thomas Nelson, 2018.

situation you are in. But just how powerful are these spirits? Let's go back to the vision the Apostle John had in the Book of Revelation—"Its tail swept a third of the stars out of the sky and flung them to earth." The stars referred to here are angels. One-third of the angels are now demons in Satan's army. And just how powerful are they?

> *Then the angel of the LORD went out and put to death a hundred and eighty-five thousand in the Assyrian camp.*
>
> *Isaiah 37:36 NIV*

One angel did that. One. And we are battling fallen angels. We'll cover more about what they can and can't do in Chapter 9, but just know for now that you can't fight them in your own strength. That's where the Holy Spirit and authority come in. We'll discuss more on authority in Chapter 7, but for now, let's focus on the Spirit.

> *But when they cried out to the LORD, he raised up for them a deliverer, Othniel son of Kenaz, Caleb's younger brother, who saved them. The Spirit of the LORD came on him, so that he became Israel's judge and went to war. The LORD gave Cushan-Rishathaim king of Aram into the hands of Othniel, who overpowered him.*
>
> *Judges 3:9–10 NIV*

> *Then the Spirit of the LORD came on Gideon, and he blew a trumpet, summoning the Abiezrites to follow him.*
>
> *Judges 6:34 NIV*

> *Then the Spirit of the LORD came upon Jephthah. He crossed Gilead and Manasseh, passed through Mizpah of Gilead, and from there he advanced against the Ammonites.*
>
> Judges 11:29 NIV

In these three examples, Scripture tells us the Spirit of the LORD came upon Othniel, Gideon, and Jephthah. In all three examples, it was to prepare them for battle. To empower them to a victorious battle. There are other examples as well—Sampson, Saul, and David, to name a few more. The Holy Spirit worked through all of them to accomplish victory. In the New Testament, when the disciples had the Holy Spirit with them and living in them after Pentecost, they were also able to accomplish great things, such as healing and casting out demons, or, more specifically, the Spirit was able to accomplish great things through them.

Have you ever stopped and asked yourself—"Why aren't these great works being accomplished today? What happened to the Holy Spirit? Has the Holy Spirit become diluted?" This is a question that I have asked myself many times. I think there are several factors at play here. First and foremost, there is the matter of faith. Let's look at the account of the demon-possessed boy in the Gospel of Matthew:

> *When they came to the crowd, a man approached Jesus and knelt before him. "Lord, have mercy on my son," he said. "He has seizures and is suffering greatly. He often falls into the fire or into the water. I brought him to your disciples, but they could not heal him." "You unbelieving and perverse generation," Jesus replied, "how long shall I stay with you? How long shall I put up with you? Bring the boy here to*

me." Jesus rebuked the demon, and it came out of the boy, and he was healed at that moment. Then the disciples came to Jesus in private and asked, "Why couldn't we drive it out?" He replied, "Because you have so little faith. Truly I tell you, if you have faith as small as a mustard seed, you can say to this mountain, 'Move from here to there,' and it will move. Nothing will be impossible for you."

Matthew 17:14-20 NIV. (Some manuscripts also include words similar to Mark 9:29 here as verse 21.)

No, I don't believe the Holy Spirit has been diluted in any way. Great works like this can still happen today. It comes down to faith. The second factor is these things *are* still happening today! Of course, it's not really reported on the news, and many churches seem to shy away from spiritual warfare altogether. The Holy Spirit is doing great and powerful things. You just don't hear about it on the five o'clock news and probably don't see much of it in your newsfeed.

The earth is the LORD's, and everything in it, the world, and all who live in it; for he founded it on the seas and established it on the waters.

Psalm 24:1 NIV

Every good and perfect gift is from above, coming down from the Father of the heavenly lights, who does not change like the shifting shadows.

James 1:17 NIV

There are two very important things to glean from these verses—Everything and everyone in the world are from God and belong to God. They belong to Him. And every good thing comes from God. And He does not change. Since this is true, the miracles of the Bible are still happening today. And with advances in medicine, miraculous healings still happen. And since they are good, they do come from God, since everything good comes from Him. The Holy Spirit certainly works through individuals to accomplish these things.

All throughout His ministry, Jesus taught His disciples. Not only teachings through parables but by example. The disciples saw Jesus heal the sick. They saw Him cast out demons. And when Jesus sent out His disciples, He told them to do this:

*Heal the sick, raise the dead, cleanse
those who have leprosy, drive out demons.
Freely you have received, freely give.*

Matthew 10:8 NIV

And in the great commission, Jesus told them this:

*All authority in heaven and on earth has been given
to me. Therefore go and make disciples of all nations,
baptizing them in the name of the Father and of
the Son and of the Holy Spirit, and teaching them
to obey everything I commanded you. And surely
I am with you always, to the very end of the age.*

Matthew 28:18-20 NIV

The Gospel of Mark puts it this way:

*Go into all the world and preach the gospel to all
creation. Whoever believes and is baptized will
be saved, but whoever does not believe will be*

condemned. And these signs will accompany those who believe: In my name they will drive out demons, they will speak in new tongues; they will pick up snakes with their hands, and when they drink deadly poison, it will not hurt them at all. They will place their hands on sick people, and they will get well.

Mark 16:15–18 NIV

If these things aren't evident to Christian believers in the world today, then the issue isn't with the Father, the Son, or the Holy Spirit, because God never changes.

Jesus Christ is the same yesterday and today and forever.

Hebrews 13:8 NIV

Yes, my friends, the Holy Spirit is still alive and well, doing great works through brothers and sisters all over the world, just as He always has and always will. It really comes down to *us*. I have seen healing take place through prayer and rebuke. I have seen spiritual attack cease through prayer and rebuke. It just takes faith and belief in the One who told us to do these things. Let's go back to our prayer to increase our faith:

Heavenly Father, Lord Jesus, Holy Spirit—I praise You for who You are. God Almighty—the creator of Heaven and earth, and my creator. You are my creator, and You created me in Your image. Thank You, God, for Your never-ending and unconditional love for me. Jesus, I ask You now to fill me with Your Holy Spirit. Heal and restore faith in me, Jesus. Grow faith in me, Jesus; increase faith in me. I love You, I trust You, I believe You, Jesus. Restore faith in me, Jesus. Strengthen my faith, Jesus. You are the author and perfector of my faith, Jesus. Open my heart to receive faith from You, Jesus. I love You, Jesus, and I ask this in Your name.

Amen.

Trusting in Jesus and having faith in the power of the Holy Spirit is essential to overcoming spiritual attacks. I encourage you to read through the Book of Judges, but most specifically Chapters 6 and 7 about Gideon. He described himself as the least in his family, which was the weakest clan in Manasseh. But God chose Gideon to lead an attack against Midian, and when the Holy Spirit was upon him, he was victorious.

Next, let's look at prayer and fasting.

CHAPTER 6

Preparing Yourself for the Fight
Prayer and Fasting

Prayer

> *Do not be anxious about anything, but in every situation, by prayer and petition, with thanksgiving, present your requests to God.*
>
> *Philippians 4:6 NIV*

Prayer, in its simplest form, is talking with God. Having a conversation with Him. Acknowledging Him for who He is, praising Him, confessing to Him, thanking Him, asking Him, and listening to Him. Prayer is the belief that God is the creator of the universe, and as such, He is our creator and hears and responds to our prayers.

Sometimes people are unsure how to pray or may feel uncomfortable praying. Jesus Himself gives us instructions on how we should pray.

> *But when you pray, go into your room, close the door and pray to your Father, who is unseen. Then your Father, who sees what is done in secret, will reward you.*
>
> *Matthew 6:6 NIV*

Is Jesus saying never to pray in public? No. But He is telling us there is something intimate about prayer.

> *And when you pray, do not keep on babbling like pagans, for they think they will be heard because of their many words. Do not be like them, for your Father knows what you need before you ask him.*
>
> Matthew 6:7–8 NIV

Does Jesus condemn lengthy prayer here? Not at all. But we should not just drone on and on with empty words. Sometimes, very short and simple prayers are the most heartfelt, and heartfelt prayers will be the most effective. Sometimes a prayer as simple as saying His name— "Jesus"—can redirect us when we are feeling scattered and bring Him back into focus. Something as simple as "Help" when you desperately need help and don't know how to put it into words or in a situation where you don't have time.

Jesus sums up His teaching on prayer with an example for us, commonly known as The Lord's Prayer.

> *After this manner therefore pray ye: Our Father which art in Heaven, Hallowed be thy name. Thy kingdom come, thy will be done in earth, as it is in heaven. Give us this day our daily bread. And forgive us our debts, as we forgive our debtors. And lead us not into temptation, but deliver us from evil: For thine is the kingdom, and the power, and the glory for ever. Amen.*
>
> Matthew 6:9–13 KJV

I used the King James translation here, as it is probably the most familiar translation for this prayer. Jesus clearly lays out a progression for our prayers. We start with addressing God and acknowledging Him as sovereign—The Almighty

God. We then proclaim that His kingdom and His will be done rather than our own. We then ask for our needs and desires—we bring our petitions to Him. We then ask for forgiveness, and we ask to have hearts to forgive others as well. Next, we ask for protection and deliverance from evil. Finally, we again declare His kingdom and power and glory forever.

Remember, when Jesus instructed His disciples how to pray, the Holy Spirit had not yet come permanently on the disciples, although Jesus did later instruct them to ask for things in His name:

> *And I will do whatever you ask in my name, so that the Father may be glorified in the Son. You may ask me for anything in my name, and I will do it.*
>
> *John 14:13–14 NIV*

And Jesus immediately follows this with the promise of the Holy Spirit:

> *If you love me, keep my commands. And I will ask the Father, and he will give you another advocate to help you and be with you forever—the Spirit of Truth. The world cannot accept him, because it neither sees him nor knows him. But you know him, for he lives with you and will be in you.*
>
> *John 14:15–17 NIV*

The Apostle Paul also instructs us to pray in the Holy Spirit.

> *And pray in the Spirit on all occasions with all kinds of prayers and requests. With this in mind, be alert and always keep praying for all the Lord's people.*
>
> Ephesians 6:18 NIV

So, what does it mean to pray in the Spirit? It simply means letting the Holy Spirit lead you in prayer. So often, we don't even know how to put into words what to pray for or exactly how to ask for it. This is why we pray in the Spirit. Ask the Holy Spirit to lead you.

> *In the same way, the Spirit helps us in our weakness. We do not know what we ought to pray for, but the Spirit himself intercedes for us through wordless groans. And he who searches our hearts knows the mind of the Spirit, because the Spirit intercedes for God's people in accordance with the will of God.*
>
> Romans 8:26-27 NIV

Let the Spirit lead you in prayer. Sometimes, the Spirit will lead you differently than you originally intended. Do not resist this! The Spirit is leading you into the will of God. Remember—

> *Trust in the LORD with all your heart and lean not on your own understanding; in all your ways submit to him and he will make your paths straight.*
>
> Proverbs 3:5-6 NIV

Talk to God as you would your best friend. Someone that you can share anything with.

> *LORD, our LORD, how majestic is your name in all the earth! You have set your glory in the heavens.*
>
> *Psalm 8:1 NIV*
>
> *Listen to my words, LORD, consider my lament. Hear my cry for help, my King and my God, for to you I pray.*
>
> *Psalm 5:1–2 NIV*
>
> *LORD, do not rebuke me in your anger or discipline me in your wrath. Have mercy on me, LORD, for I am faint; heal me, LORD, for my bones are in agony. My soul is in deep anguish. How long, LORD, how long?*
>
> *Psalm 6:1–3 NIV*

The Psalms are beautiful examples of people pouring their hearts out to God. Sometimes in joyous praise and thanksgiving, but other times in great pain and sorrow. In Psalm 6, we see the anguish that David was in. He didn't hold anything back. He shared exactly how and what he was feeling with God, as you would with a good and trustworthy friend.

And Jesus does call us His friends.

> *My command is this: Love each other as I have loved you. Greater love has no one than this: to lay down one's life for one's friends. You are my friends if you do what I command. I no longer call you servants, because a servant does not know his master's business. Instead, I have called you friends, for everything that I learned from my Father I have made known to you.*
>
> *John 15:12–15 NIV*

There is more on prayer coming up in Chapter 10. But please don't think you have to withhold anything from God or try to be fancy when you pray. He wants to hear from you, from your heart. He created you. He created your inmost being. He knows you intimately. So do not be ashamed to show yourself to Him, exactly who you are, and everything you are feeling. He made you, remember? He knows you! Should you show reverence and respect? Absolutely! He is God! But even if you are angry, you can share it with Him. Even if you are angry with Him, you can share it with Him. He is God. He can handle your anger. He can handle anything you bring to Him. He already knows your heart and how you are feeling. So just share it with Him.

Fasting

> *When you fast, do not look somber as the hypocrites do, for they disfigure their faces to show others they are fasting. Truly I tell you, they have received their reward in full. But when you fast, put oil on your head and wash your face, so that it will not be obvious to others that you are fasting, but only to your Father, who is unseen; and your Father, who sees what is done in secret, will reward you.*
>
> Matthew 6:16–18 NIV

Notice that Jesus says here, "when you fast," not "if you fast." And note that Jesus teaches about fasting just a few verses after He taught in Matthew 6:7–13 about prayer. It is part of the same teaching that is known as the Sermon on the Mount. He went immediately from teaching about prayer to teaching about fasting. Jesus expects fasting to be part of our walk with Him.

Blogger and author Nadia Thomas gives a great definition of fasting:

> *What is the definition of Christian fasting? Christian fasting is the act of intentionally abstaining from food or a regularly enjoyed good gift from God to focus on a period of spiritual growth or deepening our relationship with God. In the act of fasting, we humbly deny the flesh to focus on and glorify God, become more in tune with His Spirit, and go deeper in our prayer life.*[13]
>
> *Nadia Thomas*

And while Jesus did teach about fasting, we know that the disciples did not fast while Jesus was with them.

> *Then John's disciples came and asked him, "How is it that we and the Pharisees fast often, but your disciples do not fast?" Jesus answered, "How can the guests of the bridegroom mourn while he is with them? The time will come when the bridegroom will be taken from them; then they will fast."*
>
> *Matthew 9:14–15 NIV*

But Jesus did fast. Immediately after being baptized, Jesus was led by the Spirit into the wilderness for 40 days of fasting, which actually strengthened Him spiritually for the temptation that was coming.

---

[13] Thomas, N. Christian Fasting: Definition, Biblical Examples, & How-to. Retrieved from *https://justdisciple.com/christian-fasting/*

> *Then Jesus was led by the Spirit into the wilderness to be tempted by the devil. After fasting forty days and forty nights, he was hungry.*
>
> Matthew 4:1–2 NIV

Why do I bring this up—that we see Jesus fasting and not the disciples? I believe fasting, coupled with prayer, are important weapons in our fight against spiritual warfare. In Chapter 5, we looked at the account of Jesus driving a demon out of a boy, as told in the Book of Matthew. So let's look again at the account of the demon-possessed boy, this time from the Gospel of Mark:

> *When they came to the other disciples, they saw a large crowd around them and the teachers of the law arguing with them. As soon as all of the people saw Jesus, they were overwhelmed with wonder and ran to greet him.*
>
> *"What are you arguing about?" he asked.*
>
> *A man in the crowd answered, "Teacher, I brought you my son, who is possessed by a spirit that has robbed him of speech. Whenever it seizes him, it throws him to the ground. He foams at the mouth, gnashes his teeth, and becomes rigid. I asked your disciples to drive out the spirit, but they could not."*
>
> *"You unbelieving generation," Jesus replied, "how long shall I stay with you? How long shall I put up with you? Bring the boy to me."*

So they brought him. When the spirit saw Jesus, it immediately threw the boy into a convulsion. He fell to the ground and rolled around, foaming at the mouth.

Jesus asked the boy's father, "How long has he been like this?"

"From childhood," he answered. "It has often thrown him into the fire or water to kill him. But if you can do anything, take pity on us and help us."

"If you can?" said Jesus. "Everything is possible for one who believes."

Immediately the boy's father exclaimed, "I do believe; help me overcome my unbelief!"

When Jesus saw the crowd was running to the scene, he rebuked the impure spirit. "You deaf and mute spirit," he said, "I command you, come out of him and never enter him again."

The spirit shrieked, convulsed him violently and came out. The boy looked so much like a corpse that many said, "He's dead." But Jesus took him by the hand and lifted him to his feet, and he stood up.

After Jesus had gone indoors, his disciples asked him privately, "Why couldn't we drive it out?"

He replied, "This kind can only come out by prayer and fasting."

Mark 9:14–29 NIV

There is a lot to unpack here! But first and foremost, let's look at what Jesus said in verse 29: *He replied, "This kind can come out only by prayer and fasting."* Now, not all manuscripts and translations contain *fasting*. Some say only prayer. There is great debate on whether or not fasting was included in the original text and then later deleted or if it was never included in the original text and then added. But we do know the disciples could not drive out this spirit. We do know that they prayed, but we also know that they did not fast. We do know that Jesus both prayed and fasted.

Whether fasting was included in the original text or not, we do know by the words of Jesus that fasting is expected of us when He said, "When you fast," not "If you fast." And if some spirits can only be rebuked and driven out with fasting, then I'm in. I must admit that fasting has not been a part of my Christian walk until recently. In fact, I started fasting because of the research I uncovered while writing this book. I can say, though, I have found that fasting truly strengthens me. I find it restores me and builds my union with God. The time I would usually have spent eating a meal has been spent instead on communing with God—praying in the Spirit and reflecting on my motivation for fasting. We'll cover more on motivation for fasting shortly.

And it may be not so much the fast itself but the sacrifice that is fasting. Fasting is a surrender. It is denying our flesh in order to build our dependence on Jesus.

I look at the boy's father in this story, crying out, "I do believe," then immediately following that with, "Help me overcome my unbelief!" How many times have I found myself there—believing the lies over the promises of God? The evil one is the father of all lies. He comes to steal, kill, and destroy. Again, that is why spending time in God's word every day is so important. Let His truth, the only real truth, be written on your heart. Spend time in prayer with Him every day. Pray for Jesus to help you with your belief, just as this boy's father did. Cry out to Him. Confess your unbelief to Him, and ask Him to strengthen your belief, your trust, your faith, and your hope in Him. Ask Him daily to heal and restore your union with Him because our union with God gets attacked every day. Every single day.

And fasting does not necessarily mean giving up food. When you give up anything that you enjoy for a period of time and replace the time usually spent with that meal or activity as time spent instead with God, that is a spiritual fast. For example, you may fast from social media. You may fast from streaming your favorite show.

> *Is this the kind of fast I have chosen, only a day for people to humble themselves? Is it only for bowing one's head like a reed and for lying in sackcloth and ashes? Is that what you call a fast, a day acceptable to the LORD? Is this not the kind of fasting I have chosen: to loose the chains of injustice and untie the cords of the yoke, to set the oppressed free and break every yoke?*
>
> Isaiah 58:5–6 NIV

"Even now," declares the LORD, "return to me with all your heart, with fasting and weeping and mourning."

Joel 2:12 NIV

There can be several reasons and motivations for fasting, but also wrong motivations for fasting as well. At JustDisciple.

com, Nadia Thomas gives us some great insight into the motivations for fasting:

> *It's important to know your motivation behind fasting and to ask yourself what the purpose of the fast is. Fasting gives the Lord more room to work in our lives because we are actively emptying ourselves, thus opening more doors for us to see the Holy Spirit working in and through our lives.*
>
> Some Wrong Motivations for Fasting Include:
>
> – To be seen by others.
> – To be commended to God.
> – To be justified by God.
> – To be more holy or righteous.
> – For a reward.
>
> Some Right Motivations for Fasting Include:
>
> – For God's intervention.
> – For humility.
> – For repentance.
> – To break demonic bondage.
> – To deepen spiritual hunger for God.
> – For clarity on a decision you have to make.
> – To test and see what desires control us.[14]
>
> Nadia Thomas

---

[14] Thomas, N. Christian Fasting: Definition, Biblical Examples, & How-to. Retrieved from *https://justdisciple.com/christian-fasting/*

> *Without a purpose and a plan, it's not Christian fasting; it's just going hungry.*
>
> *John Piper*[15]

Friends, have a plan when you fast. Know why you are fasting, and fast with a true heart.

Now that we better understand the roles of prayer and fasting, let's move on to understanding our authority.

---

[15] Thomas, N. Christian Fasting Rules, Guidelines, and Best Practices. Retrieved from *https://justdisciple.com/fasting-rules/*

CHAPTER 7

Preparing Yourself for the Fight
Understanding Your Authority

Christ's Authority

> *Therefore God exalted him to the highest place and gave him the name that is above every name, that at the name of Jesus every knee should bow, in heaven and on earth and under the earth, and every tongue acknowledge that Jesus Christ is Lord, to the glory of God the Father.*
>
> Philippians 2:9–11 NIV

> *Then Jesus came to them and said, "All authority in heaven and on earth has been given to me."*
>
> Matthew 28:18 NIV

All authority in heaven and on earth has been given to Jesus. Jesus has all authority. *All authority.* His name is above all names. He has the final say on everything, and everyone and everything must submit to Him. Everyone and everything. There are no exceptions here.

Jesus tells His disciples that He has all authority as the very first part of the great commission. He then goes on to say:

> *Therefore go and make disciples of all nations, baptizing them in the name of the Father and of the Son and the Holy Spirit, and teaching them to obey everything I have commanded you.*
>
> Matthew 28:19-20 NIV

So, we understand our roles as followers of Christ. We are to go into the world and share the good news of Jesus. And what assurance does Jesus then give them?

> *… And surely I am with you always, to the very end of the age.*
>
> Matthew 28:20 NIV

Jesus first tells us clearly that He has all authority, then tells us to obey everything He commanded us to do, and then assures us that He is with us. Always with us. And one of the things that He commanded His disciples was this:

> *Heal the sick, raise the dead, cleanse those who have leprosy, drive out demons. Freely you have received, freely give.*
>
> Matthew 10:8 NIV

What else does Jesus have to say about this?

> *Now is the time for judgment on this world; now the prince of this world will be driven out.*
>
> John 12:31 NIV

Jesus is speaking to a group of people here, explaining to them that He will be crucified. God speaks to the crowd as well, in a thundering voice. But again, Jesus reassures everyone that although Satan is coming for Him, Satan has no hold over Him. And again, a few chapters later, He reassures His disciples:

> *I will not say much more to you, for the prince of this world is coming. He has no hold over me.*
>
> John 14:30 NIV

And again, in John 16, Jesus tells His disciples:

> *Because the prince of this world now stands condemned.*
>
> John 16:11 NIV

Jesus clearly tells us that Satan has no power over Him, no hold over Him whatsoever. In fact, earlier in John, Jesus clearly states that no one, including Satan, is taking His life from Him, but rather, He is giving it:

> *The reason my Father loves me is that I lay down my life—only to take it up again. No one takes it from me, but I lay it down of my own accord. I have authority to lay it down, and authority to take it up again.*
>
> John 10:17–18 NIV

Our Authority

> *The God of peace will soon crush*
> *Satan under your feet.*
>
> *Romans 16:20 NIV*

Let's look back at two key things in Matthew Chapter 28:

> *Then Jesus came to them and said, "All authority in heaven and on earth has been given to me."*
>
> *Matthew 28:18 NIV*

> *"... And surely I am with you always, to the very end of the age."*
>
> *Matthew 28:20 NIV*

Jesus has all authority. And He is with us. So, since Jesus is with us, His *authority* is also with us.

The first thing we need to truly understand is that Jesus has all authority. We do not do things in our own authority. The authority of Jesus has been delegated to us through Christ in us. As Matthew Chapter 10 tells us, it has been freely given to us. It is by the authority of Jesus and through His authority that we do things in His name.

> *I can do all things through Christ who strengthens me.*
>
> *Philippians 4:13 NKJV*

Now I will admit that this verse from Paul in Philippians is quite often taken out of context. It is often proclaimed on a job search, a sporting event, or a myriad of other situations. The context in which Paul writes to the Philippians is actually this—he was in prison at the time. He shared with the church in Philippi that he learned to be content in every situation. He had had plenty and had had nothing. He had been well-fed, and he had been hungry. The secret to his contentment? He can do all things through Christ, who gives him strength.

That's the true context of this verse. But does that mean that we are taking it out of context to say that Jesus gives us His strength and authority to rebuke demons? I don't think so. We certainly can't do it in our own strength, and we alone don't have the authority to do it. We can only do it through Jesus, and, as Paul was content in prison, we can be content in all situations, even in situations of spiritual attack, that Jesus is with us and that He has given us His strength and His authority.

Jesus also tells us:

> *And these signs will accompany those who believe: In my name they will drive out demons;*
>
> Mark 16:17 NIV

> *I have given you authority to trample on snakes and scorpions and to overcome all the power of the enemy; nothing will harm you. However, do not rejoice that the spirits submit to you, but rejoice that your names are written in heaven.*
>
> Luke 10:19–20 NIV

Friends, these words of Jesus assure us of the authority that we have through our faith in Him! His words encourage us to be bold and confident, knowing that we are empowered and protected by Him. But we must never forget that our primary focus must remain on our relationship with Jesus.

Paul tells us in 2 Corinthians:

> *For though we live in the world, we do not wage war as the world does. The weapons we fight with are not the weapons of the world. On the contrary, they have the divine power to demolish strongholds.*
>
> 2 Corinthians 10:3-4 NIV

And John tells us this:

> *You, dear children, are from God and have overcome them, because the one who is in you is greater than the one who is in the world.*
>
> 1 John 4:4 NIV

The One who is in you. Jesus has all authority. Authority over the entire universe. Everything. And as a believer, He lives in you! Let's look at a few more verses just to solidify this in our hearts.

> *But you will receive power when the Holy Spirit comes on you;*
>
> Acts 1:8 NIV

> *No, in all these things we are more than conquerors through him who loved us.*
>
> Romans 8:37 NIV

> *And God raised us up with Christ and seated us with him in the heavenly realms in Christ Jesus.*
>
> Ephesians 2:6 NIV

> *Now you are the body of Christ, and each one of you is a part of it.*
>
> 1 Corinthians 12:27 NIV

> *I have been crucified with Christ and I no longer live, but Christ lives in me. The life I now live in the body, I live by faith in the Son of God, who loved me and gave himself for me.*
>
> Galatians 2:20 NIV

> *Now if we are children, then we are heirs—heirs of God and co-heirs with Christ, if indeed we share in his sufferings in order that we may also share in his glory.*
>
> Romans 8:17 NIV

> *I have given them the glory that you gave me, that they may be one as we are one—I in them, and you in me.*
>
> John 17:22-23 NIV

As believers, the One who is in us is Jesus, and He *is greater* than the one who is in the world. We are more than conquerors through Jesus. We can not only conquer, but we can also have life to the full as God intended for us and Jesus came to give us.

Next, let's understand and take up the armor of God.

CHAPTER 8

Preparing Yourself for the Fight
The Armor of God

The Armor of God

Finally, be strong in the Lord and in his mighty power. Put on the full armor of God, so that you can take your stand against the devil's schemes. For our struggle is not against flesh and blood, but against the rulers, against the authorities, against the powers of this dark world and against the spiritual forces of evil in the heavenly realms. Therefore put on the full armor of God, so that when the day of evil comes, you may be able to stand your ground, and after you have done everything, to stand. Stand firm then, with the belt of truth buckled around your waist, with the breastplate of righteousness in place, and with your feet fitted in the readiness that comes with the gospel of peace. In addition to all this, take up the shield of faith, with which you can extinguish the arrows of the evil one. Take the helmet of salvation and the sword of the Spirit, which is the word of God.

> *And pray in the Spirit on all occasions with all kinds of prayers and requests. With this in mind, be alert and always keep praying for all the Lord's people.*
>
> Ephesians 6:10–18 NIV

I trust that most of you are probably familiar with the term *The Armor of God*. But have you really taken time to break down what Paul shared in his letter to the church in Ephesus? The first thing I will point out is that Paul tells *us* to be strong in the Lord and *His* mighty power. Then Paul tells *us* to put on the armor of God. He did not say that God will armor us. It is our responsibility to put this armor on ourselves. God has provided it for us—it is *His* armor, but we must make the choice to take it up and put it on.

Another thing that Paul points out here is—our struggle is not with the world. Our struggle and fight occur in the spiritual realm, and it is against evil. This is spiritual warfare. Satan is waging war against us, and we must prepare ourselves for the battle. Paul did not say to do this if struggles come. Just in case of struggle, just in case of warfare, here's what to do. In case of fire, break glass. No. He definitively says our struggle *is* with evil, not that we maybe, just maybe, may happen to run into it. Peter has the same definitive assertion: He says:

> *Be alert and be of sober mind. Your enemy the devil prowls around like a roaring lion looking for someone to devour. Resist him, standing firm in the faith, because you know that the family of believers throughout the world is undergoing the same kind of suffering.*
>
> 1 Peter 5:8–9 NIV

Like Paul, Peter is not saying if the devil happens to prowl around. No. He asserts that the devil *prowls* around and that he is attacking believers around the world, not that he may prowl around and that he may attack believers. No ifs here, either. And Peter says we should know this.

Something else to take note of here—in both passages, Paul and Peter tell us to *be alert*. The Greek word Paul uses here is *Agrupneo*—to be sleepless, to keep awake, to be attentive and ready. The Greek word Peter uses is *Gregoreuo*—to give strict attention to in order to avoid calamity. Jesus uses these same Greek words in the Gospels to describe how we should watch for His return.

Let's take a look at each piece of the armor and just what we, as believers, need to do to take it up.

The Belt of Truth

… *with the belt of truth buckled around your waist.*

The two main points I want to cover here are (1) knowing God's truth and (2) living in truth. In Chapter 3, we covered union with God, listening to and for God, and knowing that God's truth is in His word. If we are ever in doubt, Scripture is always the place to go to know God's truth. God's truth may and many times will conflict with the worldview. Many times, it will conflict with what your friends and family are telling you. Many times, it will conflict with our own feelings and emotions. It may even conflict with some beliefs we have held for our entire lives. But this is not a bad thing! It is an opportunity to grow closer to God!

God's truth *is* truth. And we must do our best every day to live in God's truth. Not the truth as defined by the world, our friends, our family, or our emotions or feelings. We must choose to live in God's truth. But we must do this in a way that also reflects God's forgiveness, love, patience, and kindness. Several times I have seen believers literally standing on a street corner, yelling through a megaphone, yelling at everyone around them that they are sinners destined for a fiery eternity. And I wonder—how is that working for them? To borrow a term from my friend Trent Renner— "Are they changing the population of heaven and hell?" Are they speaking truth? Well, in the fact that Jesus is the way, the truth, and the life, then yes, they are speaking the truth. But how effective is the truth they are sharing? Are they changing hearts and lives with this approach? Yes, many times Jesus got in people's faces, and quite sternly. But the faces He got in were those of the religious elite—those who held their interpretation of the law above the loving way God gave the law. Jesus approached people with love. He approached them where they were. For the most part, God has proven himself to be very gentle with us. We need to be gentle with others as well.

The other part of living in truth is—well, to be truthful! Any time we lie, we are not living in truth. And why do we lie? Well, looking at myself, it will be to hide something I have done or try to get my way with something. In me, lying can most times be directly connected with pride, shame, greed, or selfishness. My truth over God's truth. But time and time again, through His loving kindness, I am convicted of untruthfulness through the Holy Spirit. Other times, when I hold out in selfish stubbornness, God will lovingly correct me. The corrections can be painful. But they are *loving* corrections. God loves me and wants better for me. Oh, how much easier it is when I confess to being untruthful *before* God corrects me!

So what about the little white lies? I am taken back to the 80s sitcom *Married ... with Children*.[16] The wife, Peg, asks her husband, Al, "Does this dress make me look fat?" Al looks at Peg and says, "It's not the dress that makes you look fat; it's the fat that makes you look fat." And, while I did get a chuckle out of that, Al didn't lie. He told the truth. And had it not been a sitcom where Peg just gives him a dirty look, this probably would have devasted a wife in real life. So, what do we do in situations where we may be inclined to tell the little white lie? Were it me in that situation (and husbands, we have all been in that situation), I would speak the truth. "Honey, you look beautiful." But what about something trickier? Suppose a good friend had you over for dinner. You didn't really like the food and think it could have been better. Then they ask you, "Well, what do you think?"

> *Do not let any unwholesome talk come out of your mouth, but only what is helpful for building others up according to their needs, that it may benefit those who listen.*
>
> Ephesians 4:29 NIV
>
> *The tongue has the power of life and death.*
>
> Proverbs 18:21 NIV

Well, for starters, you don't have to say anything. That is not lying. I often think about my kids in such situations. When they were young and had made me something, maybe something to eat for Father's Day, something that they were so proud of, I was proud of them! To me, it was beautiful! And

---
[16] *Married ... with Children*, created by Michael G. Moye, Ron Leavitt, Fox, 1987–1997.

I loved that they did that just for me! And I told them that I loved it because I did. I loved that they did it for me. But back to the friend—if you can't find the love and beauty in the meal that you are sharing with them, you can still be encouraging but truthful to your friend—"It is a wonderful dish, a great presentation, but I'm just not a big fan of ..." whether it be fish, a certain spice, whatever the case may be.

I do most (ok all) of the cooking in our house. I love to cook, while my wife gets no pleasure from cooking whatsoever. But we both do love food! I can usually tell when I fix something that she is not a fan of. Instead of cleaning her plate, she usually has a few bites and pushes it around on her plate. When I ask her about it, she gives me loving truth. "Yeah, it's good ..." She knows that I like it, and I was excited for her to try it. But not everyone has the same tastebuds. But when she really likes something that I make, I don't even have to ask. She just tells me, "Oh my gosh, this is so good!"

That goes for everything. Do you ever stop to think about how God made us all in His image but all wonderfully unique as well? The same ingredients are in each dish. I like it, my wife, not so much. Our taste buds are different. And the same is true for me—there may be things that others like that I'm not a fan of. I believe this doesn't just stop with the sense of taste. Two people can smell the same perfume—to one; it is a beautiful fragrance. To another, well, it just stinks. Our sense of smell is different. Music can be the same—the same song heard by two different people; to one, it is a beautiful melody. To another, it's just noise. Sense of sight? The same thing applies here as well. One may see a cityscape lit up at night and see the beauty in the lights. To another, well, maybe they prefer a view of mountains or of the ocean. There is no right and wrong with our senses. We are all unique. And God made us this way! We shouldn't have to lie about little things like this. My wife knows this and tells me, "Yeah, it's good …" She may also add something like, "That's very spicy!" She appreciates that I cooked for her. But when I just get "Yeah, it's good …" well, that dish doesn't make it into the rotation. If she lied about it and said she really liked it, she may have to endure it over and over. The truth is always better than a little white lie.

While eating dinner with some friends many years ago, the wife had prepared eggplant. I had never had eggplant before, but I like almost everything, so I was anxious to try it. She put a generous portion on my plate. I'm not sure if it was the eggplant itself or maybe just the way she prepared it, but I was not a fan! To me, it tasted terrible! Not wanting to be rude, I forced down what was on my plate. She asked if I liked it, and, telling the little white lie, I said, "Yes! It's very good!" Her response? She loaded up my plate with more. The little white lies will get you!

The little white lies seem harmless. But they do give the devil a foothold. Telling the little white lies makes it easier for us to tell the big lies.

What about someone who is actually looking for constructive criticism? I used to have a manager who, once a year, would get his entire staff of about ten people together in a conference room and ask them how he could do better as a manager. I admired him for this. I admired him even more after I sat through the process. Or, I should say, after I cringed through the process. It was, at times, ruthless. Hurtful things were said, and they were meant to hurt. He sat through it, never once retaliating, never defending, but simply listening, understanding, taking notes, and repeating back to them what they had shared to make sure he had not missed anything. When my turn came, I did provide him with feedback.

I did my best to make my feedback as constructive as possible and offered alternatives to what his actions had been that I felt may have been more productive. I shared the truth but did my best to do it in such a way as to not tear him down.

In the heat of the moment, though, sometimes the truth can be difficult. So, if *truth* comes out when emotions are high, step back, and take the time to cool off. Reflect and ask yourself if it was your truth or God's truth. If it was your truth, confess this and apologize. Ask for forgiveness. If it was God's truth, reflect on that, and then you may need to confess and apologize for the way you shared it. Ask for forgiveness, and when things are calmer and cooler, and there is a safe space for sharing, use your words to express truth in a gentle, caring, and loving way that can be received by them. Be humble. Admit where you were wrong. If you were angry, apologize for your anger. If you were judgmental, apologize for being judgmental. It may be helpful to go back and re-read Chapter 4, specifically the sections on confession and repentance.

> *Instead, speaking the truth in love, we will grow to become in every respect the mature body of him who is the head, that is, Christ.*
>
> *Ephesians 4:15 NIV*

You will notice that Paul lists the belt of truth first among all other pieces of armor. I believe this is because all other pieces of the armor depend on truth.

Jesus tells us of Satan:

> *When he lies, he speaks his native language, for he is the father of lies.*
>
> *John 8:44 NIV*

Lies come from Satan; they are not of God. When we lie, we are choosing to follow Satan rather than God, though we rarely realize it in the moment. But that is what we are doing. We are choosing to lie. I said it earlier, and I will repeat it here—the very free will that God gives us is the very free will that Satan will use to attack us.

*Submit yourselves, then, to God. Resist
the devil, and he will flee from you.*

James 4:7 NIV

*Then you will know the truth, and
the truth will set you free.*

John 8:31–32 NIV

Since the truth sets us free, I do not believe it is a stretch then to say that lies will do the opposite—they will keep us in bondage to Satan. And when Satan has us in bondage, we are not in any kind of position to protect ourselves from further attack. We will tell more lies to protect the lie we've already told.

Not confessing our lies keeps us in bondage as well. The devil and his demons will continue to attack us in this very place, and it will weigh heavily on our hearts. There will be the constant fear in our hearts of being exposed. And that's exactly where the devil wants to keep us—living in fear. He can gain very powerful strongholds over our lives with fear. It can lead to stress and actually cause physical ailments.

Once the devil gets his foothold, it opens us up to believe and agree with other lies he is telling us as well. When we believe his lie that our own lies are protecting someone else's feelings, we must go back to God's truth—Satan is the father of lies. All lies come from the devil. They do not come from God. We will continue to stay in bondage if we don't step out in faith and listen to what Jesus said—the truth will set us free. We really need to take the time to meditate on this. We need to reflect on any untruth in our lives. Then ask ourselves—in this way, am I living for God or for the world? Ask the Holy Spirit to fill you and lead you. Respect others and yourself enough to speak the truth in love. You may find it helpful to go back and re-read the section on confession covered in Chapter 4.

Everyone who does evil hates the light, and will not come into the light for fear that their deeds will be exposed. But whoever lives by the truth comes into the light, so that it may be seen plainly that what they have done has been done in the sight of God.

John 3:20-21 NIV

The light shines in the darkness, and the darkness has not overcome it.

John 1:5 NIV

When we lie to others, we deceive them. Regardless of the reason, regardless of how small we think the lie is, we deceive them. When we lie to others, we are living in Satan's darkness. John 3 clearly tells us that it is the fear of being exposed that keeps us in darkness. Don't let fear keep you in the evil one's darkness. Are there things in life you are keeping hidden? Things you are keeping in the dark? If there are things in your life that you are keeping hidden, bring them into the open. Bring them into the light. Satan no longer has any hold over you when everything is in the light. There is no more fear of being exposed. Satan will use fear, uncertainty, and doubt in an attempt to always keep you in darkness. Trust in God, confess your lies to God and to those you have lied to, and come into truth, into the Kingdom of God's love and light.

This section on truth is really aimed at overcoming the lies in our *own* lives—the lies we believe and the lies we tell. It should not be interpreted that we must offer our thoughts and opinions to others on everything. James warns us about this:

> *My dear brothers and sisters, take note of this: Everyone should be quick to listen, slow to speak and slow to become angry,*
>
> James 1:19 NIV

Again, pray about these situations where you want to speak. Ask the Holy Spirit to lead you.

I know we have covered a lot here on truth. But I do believe there is a reason Paul shared this first. The belt of truth is the first thing we should always put on. We can't fully take up the rest of the armor until we are fully living in truth. If reading this is making you uncomfortable with areas in your life where you aren't being truthful, don't resist this! This is the Holy Spirit working in you! Let the Holy Spirit lead you. The devil will continue to lie and try to deceive you to get you to stay in the lie. He will tell you that the lie is the safest place to be. But Jesus wants to set you free from this bondage! Trust in Him, and He will.

The Breastplate of Righteousness

… with the breastplate of righteousness in place.

Google defines righteousness as "the quality of being morally right or justifiable." But that begs the question—being morally right or justifiable to whom? The worldview on righteousness is constantly changing and shifting. What was considered morally right 100 years ago, or even 20 years ago, no longer holds up under the modern-day scrutiny of political correctness and acceptance.

And those who define this worldview of righteousness are in a constant state of change as well. The founding fathers of the United States had their view of righteousness, and their view is seriously challenged by many today. In the United States, no, throughout the entire world, there are different powers and groups that want to define righteousness. The worldview of righteousness will very well depend on where your feet happen to be planted at any given time. What is considered righteousness in downtown San Francisco may look vastly different than what is considered righteousness in a ranching community in Montana. And both will look different than what is considered righteousness in China. Or Afghanistan. Or Africa. And in each of those locations mentioned, the current view of righteousness may look much different than it did only a few years ago. If worldview righteousness not only varies from place to place but is also ever-changing, how can we know what righteousness truly is?

But seek first his kingdom and his righteousness.

Matthew 6:33 NIV

For the LORD is our judge, the LORD is our lawgiver, the LORD is our king; it is he who will save us.

Isaiah 33:22 NIV

We know that God is the same yesterday, today, and forever. He never changes. Neither does His righteousness. And it is His righteousness that Jesus tells us to seek. When we are constantly bombarded with an ever-changing worldview of righteousness, where are we to seek and find God's righteousness?

> *For in the gospel the righteousness of God*
> *is revealed—a righteousness that is by*
> *faith from first to last, just as it is written:*
> *"The righteous will live by faith."*
>
> *Romans 1:17 NIV*
>
> *In the way of righteousness there is life;*
> *along that path is immortality.*

So let's clear up righteousness here and now, once and for all. Once someone has proclaimed Jesus as their Lord and Savior and has invited Him into their heart to live in them, they are immediately "right" with God. All sin and transgression have been erased. They are gone. These people are now righteous in God's eyes. And yes, there should be evidence of Christ now working in their lives—love, joy, peace, patience, kindness, generosity, faithfulness, gentleness, and self-control. I don't want to go down the rabbit hole of faith vs. works here. But we are righteous—seen right in God's eyes because of Jesus, not of our own works. The only work we had to do was to believe and ask Jesus to be our Lord and Savior. That is our work. Our righteousness is not of us. We can't earn it. We can't work our way into righteousness. It is a gift. Our work is to accept it. And Paul affirms that our righteousness is from Jesus:

> *Filled with the fruit of righteousness that comes through Jesus Christ—to the glory and praise of God.*
>
> Philippians 1:11 NIV

But Paul tells us to put on the full armor of God. How do we put on the righteousness that has been given to us?

> *Not having a righteousness of my own that comes from the law, but that which comes through faith in Christ—the righteousness that comes from God on the basis of faith.*
>
> Philippians 3:9 NIV

> *Abram believed the LORD, and it was credited to him as righteousness.*
>
> Genesis 15:6 NIV

If we look again at the fruits of the Spirit, we see faithfulness. Quite simply, the way we put on the breastplate of righteousness is through our faith in God. We trust Him. Even when we can't see the path, even when it isn't the direction that we want to go, we trust in God. That is faith. Faith is how we put on the breastplate of righteousness.

The Shoes of the Gospel

... and with your feet fitted in the readiness that comes with the gospel of peace.

Google defines the word *gospel* as "the teaching or revelation of Christ."[17]

---

[17] Google's English Dictionary is provided by Oxford Languages.

Encyclopedia Britannica goes deeper with background:

The word gospel is derived from the Anglo-Saxon term god-spell, meaning "good story," a rendering of the Latin evangelium and the Greek euangelion, meaning "good news" or "good telling."[18]

What does Paul mean by "feet fitted in the readiness that comes with the gospel of peace"? I believe the key word to understanding this is *readiness*. Knowing and believing the gospel or good news of Jesus makes us ready. It gives us firm footing to stand on. In fact, before Paul tells us what the armor of God is, he first tells us, *"Therefore put on the full armor of God, so that when the day of evil comes, you may be able to stand your ground, and after you have done everything, to stand. Stand firm then."* Paul says *stand* three times. Regardless of what we encounter or what we are led to do, a firm footing is required. From a practical view, shoes and boots, whether for work, play, athletics, or even dancing, are designed to provide a sure footing for the task at hand. (High heels may be the exception!) Golf shoes are designed to provide sure footing during your swing. Football and soccer players have cleats on their shoes to provide stability and maneuverability on turf. The rubber soles on the shoes of basketball players provide the same stability and maneuverability on a hardwood floor. Many jobs in industrial areas require steel-toed shoes for protection.

So how do we, as Christians, fit our feet with the sure footedness of the gospel? We spend time in it every day. We learn what Jesus taught and what He commands us to do.

---

[18] https://www.britannica.com/topic/Gospel-New-Testament

If you love me, keep my commands.

John 14:15 NIV

We won't know what Jesus teaches and commands us to do unless we spend time in Scripture, and, specifically, the four Gospels. Yes, Jesus does give us commands. But Jesus also tells us:

Come to me, all you who are weary and burdened, and I will give you rest. Take my yoke upon you and learn from me, for I am gentle and humble in heart, and you will find rest for your souls. For my yoke is easy and my burden is light.

Matthew 11:28–30 NIV

This doesn't mean we won't face tough situations. We most assuredly will. But doing what Jesus teaches us, what He commands us, isn't heavy. It will make the tough roads and paths much easier to travel when we are fitted and ready with the words of Jesus.

Have you ever noticed a single shoe lying on the side of the road? When I see them, I often think to myself, "How could someone not notice that they've lost a shoe?" It seems incomprehensible to me. Yet I think at times in our spiritual lives, we can easily lose a shoe along the way without realizing it. It is so easy to get caught up in the busyness of life and not notice things. And yes, the devil delights in such things. Spending time in Scripture daily helps us to always make sure we are tightly laced and ready to walk down any path. Take that pause every day. And any time our footing starts to seem unsure, we need to stop and check our shoes.

The Shield of Faith

In addition to all this, take up the shield of faith, with which you can extinguish the arrows of the evil one.

Let's revisit something from Chapter 5:

> *But blessed is the one who trusts in the LORD, whose confidence is in him. They will be like a tree planted by the water that sends out its roots by the stream. It does not fear when heat comes; its leaves are always green. It has no worries in a year of drought and never fails to bear fruit.*
>
> *Jeremiah 17:7–8 NIV*

Faith and trust go hand in hand. They are complementary. Our trust grows as our faith grows. And Jesus is the author and perfector of our faith. Faith is the belief in the promises of God. There are many wonderful promises that God gives us in Scripture.

> *I have come that they may have life, and have it to the full.*
>
> *John 10:10 NIV*

Having life to the full doesn't mean waiting for heaven. Jesus wants us to have life to the full now! And we can! But just before He assures us of this, Jesus gives us this warning—

> *The thief comes only to steal and kill and destroy;*
>
> *John 10:10 NIV*

Satan will do everything in his power—let me rephrase that—Satan will do everything that God allows him to do to keep us from having life to the full. And so many times, we let him. More on what Satan can and can't do is coming up in Chapter 9, but for now, know this—the devil will play the long game. He wants to slowly steal, kill, and destroy in our lives until our lives feel empty rather than full. He wants to wear us down. And because he is the father of all lies, he is so very well practiced at the art of deceiving us, slowly stealing from us the full life that God intends for us, and wearing us down. Once you learn to recognize them, you will see these subtle attacks far more often than you see the larger attacks, which can actually be easier to recognize. Remember, the devil deceives and doesn't want you to know he is actually attacking you. He will be stealthy much more often than obvious.

You may be able to look back on previous times and recognize where he has deceived you in the past. We will cover that more in Chapter 10. Remember, the devil deceives and doesn't want you to know he is actually attacking you. He will be stealthy much more often than obvious.

When describing the full armor of God, Paul says that with the shield of faith, we can extinguish the arrows of the evil one. Faith is trusting in what God has promised, and when I am able to stop and reflect on all that He has already done for me and how faithful He has been to me, it helps to get me out of my head. Back in Chapter 2, we looked at the image of a little devil over one shoulder and an angel over the other shoulder, whispering in our ears. From my experience, most spiritual attacks take place in my head. Not always, but most of the time. Before I really started researching spiritual attack, my wife and I used to call them "punks." For the most part, we still do refer to them as "the punks in my head." What is fascinating is that just by recalling what God has done in my life, I can much more easily quiet the punks. That, my friends, is very simply taking up the Shield of Faith.

For example, as I shared with you in Chapter 1, my wife and I face the same struggles that other couples face. And although every couple is unique, there are probably commonalities among couples around these struggles. Of course, the devil doesn't want you to believe that. He will get those punks in your head, telling you that your situation is hopeless and that you just aren't meant for one another. Something small can turn into something that seems insurmountable. The devil tries to convince us that these molehills are actually mountains. When I can stop and remind myself that throughout every situation, no matter how difficult it seemed at the time, God has seen us through each and every one of them. And along the way, God has revealed valuable lessons to us about ourselves. Each situation has actually been an opportunity to lean on God, trust in God, grow closer to Him, and grow closer to each other. God has turned each situation into a blessing. Scripture tells us:

> *And we know that in all things God works*
> *for the good of those who love him, who have*
> *been called according to his purpose.*
>
> *Romans 8:28 NIV*

So take up the Shield of Faith to extinguish the arrows of the enemy. Recall just how faithful God has been to you in so very many situations. I know from experience that sometimes, we get so deep in our heads that it is hard to recall these situations. We will discuss that more in the Sword of the Spirit section, as well as in Chapter 10.

The Helmet of Salvation

Take the helmet of salvation.

Perhaps the most well-known and most quoted Scripture is John 3:16—

> For God so loved the world that he gave his one and only Son, that whoever believes in him shall not perish but have eternal life.
>
> John 3:16 NIV

We see it written on signs and bumper stickers. In the late 1970s, a man by the name of Rollen Stewart was determined to "get the message out" and started holding up John 3:16 signs at televised sporting events. Those of you that are old enough may remember him—he wore a rainbow-colored afro-style wig. Rollen Stewart is currently serving three life sentences in Mule Creek State Prison for kidnapping.[19]

I don't know Mr. Stewart, and I don't know where Mr. Stewart's heart was when he did this. But my personal feeling is that the rainbow wig made him more of a spectacle than a messenger.

Let's look at another example of John 3:16 in modern culture and sports. In 2009, Tim Tebow wrote John 3:16 in the eye black beneath his eyes for the BCS National Championship game between Florida and Oklahoma, which led 90 million people to Google John 3:16.

So let's look again at John 3:16—

---

[19] *https://en.wikipedia.org/wiki/Rollen_Stewart*

> *For God so loved the world that he gave his one and only Son, that whoever believes in him shall not perish but have eternal life.*
>
> John 3:16 NIV

And that is a wonderful promise indeed! Eternal life! That, my friends, is salvation. God became flesh as Jesus through the Holy Spirit and the Virgin Mary. He lived a blameless life, and He died on the cross as an atonement for the sins of all mankind. It is a loving gift. If the devil's lies ever cause you to doubt God's love for you, remember this: God sent Jesus to die for you. That's how much He loves you. Jesus died for you. He gave His life willingly and lovingly; no one took it from Him.

> *The reason my Father loves me is that I lay down my life—only to take it up again. No one takes it from me, but I lay it down of my own accord. I have authority to lay it down and authority to take it up again. This command I received from my Father.*
>
> John 10:17–18 NIV

Jesus went to the cross and died for you. That's how much He loves you. He is with you now, and you will be with Him for eternity.

> *For I am convinced that neither death nor life, neither angels nor demons, neither the present nor the future, neither height nor depth, nor anything else in all creation, will be able to separate us from the love of God that is in Christ Jesus our Lord.*
>
> Romans 8:38–39 NIV

When we know this in our hearts and remind ourselves of this, it is easier to release the attacks of today or even the attacks of a season that you may be going through. This will pass. Eternity with Jesus is just that—eternity. An eternity with no suffering.

> *And I heard a loud voice from the throne saying, "Look! God's dwelling place is now among the people, and he will dwell with them. They will be his people, and God himself will be with them and be their God. 'He will wipe every tear from their eyes. There will be no more death' or mourning or crying or pain, for the old order of things has passed away."*
>
> *He who was seated on the throne said, "I am making everything new!" Then he said, "Write down these words, for these words are trustworthy and true."*
>
> *Revelation 21:3-5 NIV*

Yes, salvation is a wonderful promise indeed! But Paul is so specific about how he calls out the Armor of God. Salvation is our helmet. Helmets are used to protect our heads. This is an excellent reminder of exactly where most of the devil's attacks will take place. He will lie and try to get in our heads more than anything else.

The Sword of the Spirit

... and the sword of the Spirit, which is the word of God.

Paul tells us that the sword of the Spirit is the Word of God. Again, this speaks to the importance of spending time in Scripture every day. And the promises that God will write His words on our hearts really start to take on a deeper meaning here. When we have the Word of God in our hearts, we can recall these words to turn the attack around. Take it back to the devil. And always remember that God is with you at all times, even during these attacks. It will be most helpful to remind yourself of this. And to remind the devil as well.

Be strong and courageous. Do not be terrified because of them, for the LORD your God goes with you; he will never leave you nor forsake you.

Deuteronomy 31:6 NIV

And surely I am with you always, to the very end of the age.

Matthew 28:20 NIV

So just which verses may help in spiritual attacks? Well, it really depends on the attack. We will review some specific verses for specific situations when we get to Chapter 10. But know this—we do fight back with the Word of God.

Jesus Himself did this when He was tempted, and temptation is a form of attack. Let's look back at the Gospel of Matthew. Jesus had just been baptized by John the Baptist at the end of Chapter 3. Let's pick it up in Chapter 4.

Then Jesus was led by the Spirit into the wilderness to be tempted by the devil. After fasting for forty days and forty nights, he was hungry. The tempter came to him and said, "If you are the Son of God, tell these stones to become bread."

Matthew 4:1–3 NIV

Let's pause there for just a minute. At the end of Matthew Chapter 3, immediately after Jesus was baptized, Scripture tells us that the Spirit of God came to Jesus like a dove from heaven. Then God spoke:

> *And a voice from heaven said, "This is my Son, whom I love; with him I am well pleased."*
>
> *Matthew 3:17 NIV*

Notice in Matthew 4:3 that the first thing the devil does is try to question who Jesus is. "If you are the Son of God ..." The devil will certainly do that with us as well. He will try to make us question our relationship with God, try to make us question whether or not God is really with us. That's why knowing the verses that God promises to always be with us are so important to remember. But Jesus is very confident in knowing that He is the Son of God. He doesn't even respond to that, but He does answer the devil with Scripture:

> *Jesus answered, "It is written: 'Man shall not live on bread alone, but on every word that comes from the mouth of God.'"*
>
> *Matthew 4:4 NIV*

Jesus responds to Satan with words from Deuteronomy 8:3.

> *Then the devil took him to the holy city and had him stand on the highest point of the temple. "If you are the Son of God," he said, "throw yourself down. For it is written: 'He will command his angels concerning you, and they will lift you up in their hands, so that you will not strike your foot against a stone.'"*
>
> *Matthew 4:5–6 NIV*

Once again, we see the devil try to chip away at who Jesus is. Again, "If you are the Son of God." And, again, Jesus pays no attention to that. But the other thing we see here is this— the devil uses Scripture. He quotes Psalms 91:11 and 12. Yes, he does twist it to try to fit his agenda. Remember one of the most important things about the devil; he will try to deceive you by any means possible. He does know Scripture. A part of me wonders if these very verses were included in Scripture for this very moment between Jesus and the devil. And Jesus could have very well responded with the verse that immediately follows:

> *You will tread on the lion and the cobra, you will trample the great lion and the serpent.*
>
> *Psalm 91:13 NIV*

But no, Jesus is outsmarting the devil here. He is not engaging but simply rebuking what the devil is throwing at Him. He responds again with Scripture:

> *Jesus answered him, "It is also written: 'Do not put the LORD your God to the test.'"*
>
> *Matthew 4:7 NIV*

We see here that Jesus responds from Deuteronomy 6:16. Then the devil tries a different approach:

> *Again, the devil took him to a very high mountain and showed him all the kingdoms of the world and their splendor. "All of this I will give you," he said. "if you will bow down and worship me."*
>
> *Matthew 4:8–9 NIV*

The devil is no longer questioning who Jesus is. But here, we see the devil trying to appeal to the human side of Jesus. Jesus is fully God, but He is also fully human. I say the human side of Jesus because I look at my own humanity, my flesh, and my sinful nature. The devil here is offering Jesus worldly riches. But we know Jesus certainly could have possessed all worldly riches, but that is not why He came. He lived a modest and humble life on earth to serve, save, and do the will of His Father. Let's look at Jesus' response:

> *Jesus said to him, "Away from me Satan!*
> *For it is written: 'Worship the LORD*
> *your God, and serve him only.'"*

Matthew 4:10 NIV

Once again, Jesus responds with Scripture, this time from Deuteronomy 6.13. Notice that each time, Jesus responds to Satan with Scripture. The sword of the Spirit, which is the Word of God. Also, notice that each time, Jesus responds with Scripture from Deuteronomy. As Christians, it is easy at times to focus on the New Testament. And, as Christians, we should strive to learn everything that Jesus said, as He Himself said:

> *If you love me, keep my commands.*

John 14:15 NIV

But also remember this—

> *All scripture is God-breathed and is useful for teaching, rebuking, correcting and training in righteousness, so that the servant of God may be thoroughly equipped for every good work.*

2 Timothy 3:16-17 NIV

As we look back at the armor of God, we see that most pieces are defensive equipment—the belt of truth, breastplate of righteousness, shoes of the gospel of peace, shield of faith, and helmet of salvation. The only offensive weapon we have is the sword of the Spirit—the Word of God. Friends, don't try to fight the devil with anything else.

And pray in the Spirit on all occasions with all kinds of prayers and requests. With this in mind, be alert and always keep praying for all the Lord's people.

Ephesians 6:18 NIV

We covered a lot in this chapter! But, we still have one more piece of training. We need to know and understand who our battle is with.

CHAPTER 9

Preparing Yourself for the Fight
Understanding the Enemy

Knowing the Enemy

The ancient Chinese military General, strategist, philosopher, and writer Sun Tzu said:

> If you know the enemy and know yourself, you need not fear the result of a hundred battles. If you know yourself but not the enemy, for every victory gained you will also suffer defeat. If you know neither the enemy nor yourself, you will succumb in every battle.[20]

We have spent the better part of the last six chapters preparing ourselves. And along the way, I hope you have been very honest with yourself and have come to know yourself better. Now is the time to know and understand our enemy. We need to understand who the enemy is and who the enemy isn't—

> For our struggle is not against flesh and blood, but against the rulers, against the authorities, against

---

[20] Sun Tzu, *The Art of War*, Filiquarian, 2007.

> the powers of this dark world and against the spiritual forces of evil in the heavenly realms.
>
> Ephesians 6:12 NIV

Our enemy is the spiritual forces of evil. The devil and his dark kingdom.

In his book *Satan: Our Adversary the Devil*, Don Stewart sheds valuable light on seeking to learn exactly who the enemy is.

> *In our study of Satan, we should only go as far as the Bible teaches. Consequently, we should not engage in fruitless speculation about his character. The key is to find the right balance. We need to know enough about our enemy so that we can understand how he works, but we should not be obsessed about him. In fact, our study of Scripture should concentrate on those things which Scripture itself emphasizes; the character of God and our relationship to Him.*
>
> *In reality, our emphasis should always be on the Lord, not Satan because the Bible is all about Him. It is not about the devil. In fact, the devil is only mentioned in Scripture when he has played some specific part in God's story of the salvation of humanity. Otherwise he is not mentioned at all.*
>
> *Therefore, we should be careful not to speculate about this evil being. The key is to find the proper balance when looking into this subject.*
>
> *In sum, when we study about the devil, and the various ways in which he works, it should always be in the context of studying about who God is,*

as well as His overall plan for the human race. This is where our energies should be directed.[21]

Who Is Satan?

So, if Mr. Stewart says we should not speculate but look to what the Bible teaches us about Satan, what does the Bible say about Satan?

First, let's look at what the Bible tells us about who the devil is.

> *We know that we are children of God, and that the whole world is under the control of the evil one.*
>
> *1 John 5:19 NIV*

Wait, what? The whole world is under the control of the evil one? Let's look at more.

In John 14, Jesus says this about the devil—

> *I will not say much more to you, for the prince of this world is coming. He has no hold over me, but he comes so that the world may learn that I love the Father and do exactly what my Father has commanded me.*
>
> *John 14:30–31 NIV*

Yes. Jesus Himself refers to Satan as the prince of this world.

In 2 Corinthians, Paul says this of the devil—

> *The god of this age has blinded the minds of unbelievers, so that they cannot see the*

---

[21] Don Stewart, *Satan: Our Adversary the Devil*, EOW (Educating Our World), 2020.

> *light of the gospel that display the glory
> of Christ, who is the image of God.*
>
> *2 Corinthians 4:4 NIV*

The god of this age? Notice that in his second letter to the church in Corinth, Paul does use the word god, but with a lowercase "g," to describe Satan. Lowercase "g" gods are throughout the Bible. But remember, there is only one true God.

In Ephesians, Paul says this about the devil—

> *As for you, you were dead in your transgressions
> and sins, in which you used to live when you
> followed the ways of this world and the ruler
> of the kingdom of the air, the spirit who is
> now at work in those who are disobedient.*
>
> *Ephesians 2:1–2 NIV*

In his letter to the Ephesians, Paul describes Satan as the ruler of the kingdom of the air and tells us he is also the spirit that works in those who are disobedient. Our enemy is not flesh and blood, remember? Our enemy is the spirit that works in them.

So far, we have the Bible itself referring to Satan as having control of the world, the prince of this world, the god of this age, and the ruler of the kingdom of the air. Let's look at some other descriptions of Satan from the Bible.

In John Chapter 8, Jesus describes the devil in this way:

> *He was a murderer from the beginning, not holding to
> the truth, for there is no truth in him. When he lies, he
> speaks his native language, for he is the father of lies.*
>
> *John 8:44 NIV*

Jesus tells us clearly that the devil was a murderer from the beginning and calls him the father of lies. And James says this—

> *When tempted, no one should say, "God is tempting me." For God cannot be tempted by evil, nor does he tempt anyone.*
>
> James 1:13 NIV

The devil is a tempter. The devil is *the* tempter. And again, let's look at what Peter says about the devil—

> *Be alert and of sober mind. Your enemy the devil prowls around like a roaring lion looking for someone to devour.*
>
> 1 Peter 5:8 NIV

The devil is like a roaring lion, looking for someone to devour.

And you will recall this from Chapter 2—

> *The great dragon was hurled down—that ancient serpent called the devil, or Satan, who leads the whole world astray. He was hurled to the earth, and his angels with him.*
>
> Revelation 12:9 NIV

We clearly see that Satan and his fallen angels, or demons, have been hurled to the earth, and he wants to lead the whole world astray.

There is more evidence of this in 2 Corinthians—

But I am afraid that just as Eve was deceived by the serpent's cunning, your minds may somehow be led astray from your sincere and pure devotion to Christ.

2 Corinthians 11:3 NIV

The devil is also a liar, in fact, the father of all lies and a tempter. He is like a roaring lion, and he is the ancient serpent that has been doing his best to deceive us and lead us astray since the Garden of Eden.

And no wonder, for Satan himself masquerades as an angel of light. It is not surprising, then, if his servants also masquerade as servants of righteousness.

2 Corinthians 11:14–15 NIV

Satan will attempt to deceive and, at times, even appear righteous in his deceit. And, he may work through others that may also appear righteous and well-meaning. This is why it is so very important to study Scripture to reveal the truth. God will never contradict himself. Even if you are being told something that sounds true and good, if it cannot be backed up with Scripture, there is a good chance it is an attempt to deceive you.

How did Satan become the devil? The clearest biblical pictures we have come from the Books of Isaiah and Ezekiel.

How you have fallen from heaven, morning star, son of the dawn! You have been cast down to the earth, you who once laid low the nations! You said in your heart, "I will ascend to the heavens; I will raise my throne above the stars of God; I will sit enthroned on the mount of assembly, on the utmost heights of Mount Zaphon. I will make myself like the Most High."

Isaiah 14:12-14 NIV

You were the seal of perfection, full of wisdom and perfect in beauty. You were in Eden, the garden of God; every precious stone adorned you: carnelian, chrysolite and emerald, topaz, onyx and jasper, lapis lazuli, turquoise and beryl. Your settings and mountings were made of gold; on the day you were created they were prepared. You were anointed as a guardian cherub, for so I ordained you. You were on the holy mount of God; you walked among the fiery stones. You were blameless in your ways from the day you were created till wickedness was found in you. Through your widespread trade you were filled with violence, and you sinned. So I drove you in disgrace from the mount of God, and I expelled you, guardian cherub, from among the fiery stones. Your heart had become proud on account of your beauty, and you corrupted your wisdom because of your splendor. So I threw you to the earth; I made a spectacle of you before kings.

Ezekiel 28:12-17 NIV

Biblical scholars debate whether the above passages from Isaiah and Ezekiel describe the fall of Satan, or simply the fall of the king of Babylon from Isaiah, and the fall of the king of Tyre from Ezekiel, or metaphorically refer to both kings as well as Satan. But there seem to be some things in both passages that can't be attributed to a human. In Isaiah, there is a reference to morning star. Morning star is translated from

Lucifer. In fact, the King James translation of the Bible uses the name Lucifer rather than morning star in Isaiah 14:12. And in Ezekiel, there is a clear reference to the Garden of Eden, and one who was anointed and ordained as a guardian cherub, again a status that isn't attributed to a human.

Earlier in this chapter, I referenced Don Stewart's *Satan: Our Adversary*, in which Mr. Stewart cautions that we should only go as far as the Bible teaches and that we should be careful not to speculate about this evil being. Mr. Stewart does go on later in his book to comment specifically on the above passages from Isaiah and Ezekiel:

The King of Babylon (Isaiah 14)

In the Book of Isaiah, there is judgment pronounced against the King of Babylon. The description of this earthly king does not seem to fit a mere human being. This personage is called "son of dawn," or "morning star." This passage records this being saying, "I will ascend to heaven," "I will raise my throne above the stars of God" and "I will make myself like the Most High."

This appears to be describing someone other than an earthly creature. Therefore, it is widely believed that Isaiah is describing the fall of the created being who became Satan in this passage. Yet there are those who do not necessarily see this as a reference to the fall of Satan.

The King of Tyre (Ezekiel 28)

There is also judgment pronounced against the King of Tyre as recorded in the Book of Ezekiel. While referring initially to an earthly ruler, the description seems to be going beyond a mere earthly personage. He is said to be "perfect in beauty," and the "anointed cherub." It is also said of him that "he was on the holy mountain" and "he was blameless." Since this can hardly describe an earthly, pagan ruler, many think that Satan, the devil, is ultimately in view.

While there is no mention of the name Satan in these three passages, nor do they specifically speak of a non-human created being, they do seem to be referring to some created being who existed with God in the beginning and eventually became the devil.

If not, we would apparently have to assume that God created this being as sinful. However, the Bible makes it clear that everything God created was created "very good."

Consequently, it seems that we can be somewhat certain that these passages also refer to this spirit-being who was created perfect but then became Satan, the Adversary.

To sum up, we know that the devil became evil, though we may not be entirely certain how this occurred. To conclude that Satan is the personage behind the serpent in Genesis chapter three, as well as the King of Babylon in Isaiah, and the King of Tyre in the Book of Ezekiel, is consistent with the rest of Scripture, though nothing is specifically said in these passages which identifies him as a perfect created being who fell from his original state.[22]

---

[22] Don Stewart, *Satan: Our Adversary the Devil*, EOW (Educating Our World), 2020.

Regardless of how we interpret Isaiah 14 and Ezekiel 28, I think we can assume Satan is prideful. He wants to be God, but he can't. God is love. Satan is hate. God is merciful. Satan is merciless. God is justice. Satan is injustice. Satan comes to kill, steal, and destroy. God is the giver of life, blesses us, and is the creator. We know that Satan is the father of all lies, and he will attempt to deceive us at every opportunity. God is the Heavenly Father. God is truth, and He will never lie or deceive us.

All this may sound pretty daunting, right? The devil is not to be taken lightly. But let's now look at the limitations of Satan.

Who Satan Is Not

> *"Simon, Simon, Satan has asked to sift all of you as wheat. But I have prayed for you, Simon, that your faith may not fail. And when you have turned back, strengthen your brothers."*
>
> Luke 22:31–32 NIV

Notice here that Satan asked. Satan could not just do it. Yes, Satan is powerful. But in all of his power, he is still under the authority of God. He cannot do anything that God does not allow him to do. But another example, perhaps our best example, comes from the Book of Job.

> *One day the angels came to present themselves before the LORD, and Satan came with them. The LORD said to Satan, "Where have you come from?" Satan answered the LORD, "From roaming through the earth and going back and forth in it." Then the LORD*

> said to Satan, "Have you considered my servant Job? There is no one on earth like him; he is blameless and upright, a man who fears God and shuns evil."
>
> Job 1:6–8 NIV

So, the first thing to notice here—the angels appear before God, and Satan is with them. God addresses Satan, and Satan responds. God is definitely calling the shots here. Then comes God's response back to Satan, and I'll be honest with you, Job 1:8 has been one of the most troubling verses in the Bible for me. It's like God is handing Job over on a silver platter! I struggled with that for many years. But as I have grown in my Christian maturity, I have a much greater understanding of this. We'll discuss this more in Chapter 18, but for now, let's get back to Job.

> "Does Job fear God for nothing?" Satan replied?
> "Have you not put a hedge around him and his household and everything he has? You have blessed the work of his hands, so that his flocks and herds are spread throughout the land. But stretch out your hand and strike everything he has, and he will surely curse you to your face. The LORD said to Satan, "Very well, then, everything he has is in your hands, but on the man himself do not lay a finger." Then Satan went out from the presence of the LORD.
>
> Job 1:9–12 NIV

In verse 10, Satan acknowledges that God has protected Job and everything he has. Satan also acknowledges that God has blessed the work of Job's hands. Job worked for the things he had, and God blessed his work. In verse 11, Satan acknowledges again that Job and all his possessions *are* under God's protection. In verse 12, God then *allows* Satan some level of control. God puts everything Job has in Satan's hands, but God also limits Satan and does not allow him to "lay a finger" on Job himself. God IS under control of everything, including Satan. Satan only has control of what God allows him to control.

So, what kind of power does Satan actually have? As we continue in Job, we will shed light on this.

> *One day, when Job's sons and daughters were feasting and drinking wine at the oldest brother's house, a messenger came to Job and said, "The oxen were plowing and the donkeys were grazing nearby, and the Sabeans attacked and carried them off. They put the servants to the sword, and I am the only one who has escaped to tell you!"*
>
> *Job 1:13–15 NIV*

We see, in this case, that God allowed Satan the ability to entice the Sabeans to attack and kill Job's servants and plunder Job's oxen and donkeys.

> *While he was still speaking, another messenger came and said, "The fire of God fell from the sky and burned up the sheep and servants, and I am the only one who has escaped to tell you!"*
>
> *Job 1:16 NIV*

Here we see God allowed Satan the ability to cause natural (or supernatural?) disaster, killing Job's sheep and servants. Fire falling from the sky brings to mind a volcano erupting and raining down fire.

> *While he was still speaking, another messenger came and said, "The Chaldeans formed three raiding parties and swept down on your camels and carried them off. They put the servants to the sword, and I am the only one who has escaped to tell you!"*
>
> *Job 1:17 NIV*

Again, we see God allowed Satan the ability to entice a group of people, this time the Chaldeans, to attack and kill Job's servants and to plunder Job's camels.

> *While he was still speaking, yet another messenger came and said, "Your sons and daughters were feasting and drinking wine at the oldest brother's house, when suddenly a mighty wind swept in from the desert and struck the four corners of the house. It collapsed on them and they are dead, and I am the only one who has escaped to tell you!"*
>
> *Job 1:18-19 NIV*

And again, we see God allowed Satan the ability to bring about natural disaster, in the form of strong wind, to collapse the house and kill all of Job's children.

> *At this, Job got up and tore his robe and shaved his head. Then he fell to the ground in worship and said: "Naked I came from my mother's womb, and naked I will depart. The LORD gave and the LORD has taken away; may the name of God be praised." In all this, Job did not sin by charging God with wrongdoing.*
>
> *Job 1:20-22 NIV*

In all this, Job did not do as Satan anticipated he would. But Satan wasn't done yet. Or God wasn't done yet …

On another day the angels came to present themselves before the LORD, and Satan also came with them to present himself before him. And the LORD said to Satan, "Where have you come from?"

Satan answered the LORD, "From roaming throughout the earth, going back and forth on it."

Then the LORD said to Satan, "Have you considered my servant Job? There is no one on earth like him; he is blameless and upright, a man who fears God and shuns evil. And he still maintains his integrity, though you incited me against him to ruin him without any reason."

"Skin for skin!" Satan replied. "A man will give all he has for his own life. But now stretch out your hand and strike his flesh and bones, and he will surely curse you to your face."

The LORD said to Satan, "Very well, then, he is in your hands; but you must spare his life."

So Satan went out from the presence of the LORD and afflicted Job with painful sores from the soles of his feet to the crown of his head. Then Job took a piece of broken pottery and scraped himself with it as he sat among the ashes.

His wife said to him, "Are you still maintaining your integrity? Curse God and die!"

> He replied, "You are talking like a foolish woman.
> Shall we accept good from God, and not trouble?"
>
> In all this, Job did not sin in what he said.
>
> Job 2:1–10 NIV

Here we see a very similar situation. Satan once again comes before God, with God clearly in command. This time, God allowed Satan to inflict harm on Job's body, but God also restricted him from taking Job's life.

When Satan says in these verses that he has been roaming throughout the earth, Peter's warning immediately comes to mind—

> Be alert and of sober mind. Your enemy
> the devil prowls around like a roaring
> lion looking for someone to devour.
>
> 1 Peter 5:8 NIV

If you aren't familiar with the complete Book of Job, I encourage you to read it! I won't give any spoilers other than to say the devil is not mentioned again, but that doesn't mean Job's suffering immediately stops.

So, let's recap what we now know about the devil. The Bible calls him the prince of this world, the god of this age, and the ruler of the kingdom of the air. The Bible tells us that the world is under his control but also tells us that he can only do what God allows him to do. He is very powerful, can incite people against others, cause natural disasters, and inflict physical injury and pain. He is the father of all lies, is enraged, and is waging war against us. We need to know how to resist him.

Now that we better know ourselves and better know our enemy, let's move next to how we can better resist him.

CHAPTER 10

How We Fight

"Not by might nor by power, but by my Spirit," says the LORD Almighty.

Zechariah 4:6 NIV

Do not be afraid of them; the LORD your God himself will fight for you.

Deuteronomy 3:22 NIV

He shall say: "Hear, Israel: Today you are going into battle against your enemies. Do not be fainthearted or afraid; do not panic or be terrified by them. For the LORD your God is the one who goes with you to fight for you against your enemies to give you victory."

Deuteronomy 20:3–4 NIV

The LORD himself goes before you and will be with you; he will never leave you nor forsake you. Do not be afraid; do not be discouraged.

Deuteronomy 31:8 NIV

> *Have I not commanded you? Be strong and courageous. Do not be afraid; do not be discouraged, for the LORD your God will be with you wherever you go.*
>
> Joshua 1:9 NIV

As mentioned in Chapter 3, it is essential not to be afraid. But many, many times, it won't be Satan that we are actually afraid of. Instead, it will be the situation we find ourselves in. Remember, fear is a very powerful weapon in Satan's arsenal that he will use against us.

Fear, uncertainty, and doubt, abbreviated as FUD, is one of the oldest tactics in sales. Google includes the acronym FUD, and defines it as "Fear, uncertainty, and doubt, usually evoked intentionally in order to put a competitor at a disadvantage."[23] FUD has appeared in sales literature for over 100 years, but salespeople have probably been using the concept for much longer. It is one of the devil's most effective tactics. He is trying to "sell" you on the idea. He is trying to plant seeds of fear, uncertainty, and doubt. He wants you to make an agreement with it. He wants to put you at a disadvantage. We discussed agreements in Chapter 5, and it might be a good idea to go back and review that again. It is very important that we break agreements with the lies we have been told, including lies of fear, uncertainty, and doubt.

> *For God gave us a spirit not of fear but of power and love and self-control.*
>
> 2 Timothy 1:7 ESV

So, how do we overcome fear?

---

[23] Google's English Dictionary is provided by Oxford Languages.

Prayer and meditation are great ways to overcome fear. Meditation often focuses on breathing. Controlled breathing has been proven to be an excellent way to reduce stress. In fact, the U.S. Military, first responders, and many athletes use a technique called Combat Tactical Breathing. The concept is very simple—breathe in, counting 1, 2, 3, 4. Stop and hold your breath counting 1, 2, 3, 4. Then, exhale, counting 1, 2, 3, 4. Repeat this several times. There is science behind this, friends! This type of tactical breathing actually slows the sympathetic nervous system, which controls "fight-or-flight" responses in the body. And while slowing the sympathetic nervous system, tactical breathing also engages the body's parasympathetic nervous system, which controls the body's ability to relax. This is also known as "rest and digest," as opposed to "fight-or-flight."

God designed our nervous systems! In all His wisdom, goodness, and love, He gave us these nervous systems for our benefit. Sometimes, we definitely need the "fight-or-flight" to kick in. It can save us. But, as the military and first responders know, we also need to have cool heads. That can save us as well.

Breathing can indeed help with the physiological conditions of fear, uncertainty, and doubt. But fear, uncertainty, and doubt are also issues of the mind.

It's All in Your Head

Cast all your anxiety on him because he cares for you.

1 Peter 5:7 NIV

Peter tells us to give our worries and anxieties to God because He cares for us.

Anxiety and worry can consume us if we let it. In a recent church service that my wife and
I attended, the pastor spoke of the gap that lies between the known and the unknown. All too often, we can let this gap be filled with worry and anxiety. At least I can. It seems to be my default go-to. I asked my wife after this service, "Hunny, what do you worry about the most?" Her reply? "What don't I worry about?" So at least I'm not alone in this! And it seems to be shared among most if not all of us, as this was the message in church that day. I urge you to read all of Matthew Chapter 6, or better yet, all of Matthew 5–7, better known as Jesus' Sermon on the Mount. But for now, let's focus on two key verses from Matthew Chapter 6.

*Can any one of you by worrying add
a single hour to your life?*

Matthew 6:27 NIV

*But seek first his kingdom and his righteousness,
and all these things will be given to you as well.*

Matthew 6:33 NIV

This whole section of Jesus' sermon was a warning against worry. His answer instead? Seek God. Instead of filling the gap with worry, fill the gap with God.

So, how can we do that?

*Rejoice in the Lord always. I will say it again:
Rejoice! Let your gentleness be evident to all. The
Lord is near. Do not be anxious about anything,
but in every situation, by prayer and petition, with
thanksgiving, present your requests to God. And the*

peace of God, which transcends all understanding, will guard your hearts and your minds in Christ Jesus.

Finally, brothers and sisters, whatever is true, whatever is noble, whatever is right, whatever is pure, whatever is lovely, whatever is admirable—if anything is excellent or praiseworthy—think about such things.

Philippians 4:4–8 NIV

Friends, this can be hard to do. Speaking for myself, there are times that I would rather just wallow in sorrow, self-pity, or self-reproach, and sometimes a combination of all three. But when I gather the strength and courage to rejoice and think about good things, my perspective does indeed change. Yes, I must pray and ask for the strength and courage to do this. And while we can choose to just tough it out, force ourselves to pick ourselves up, and do something, it may help for a time. But typically, what we choose is only a distraction, and distractions only provide temporary relief. What we really need is healing rather than relief.

Jesus provides healing. When I stop to reflect on something true, noble, right, pure, lovely, admirable, excellent, and worthy of praise, I think back to my wedding. While the entire wedding was beautiful, there was a point in the wedding, just before we were announced "husband and wife." My wife and I were looking at each other, and my wife was literally bouncing up and down, almost jumping. There was a huge smile on her face. Her eyes shined with joy as I had never seen before. This was the purest moment of my life. When I think back on this, it reminds me just how much God loves me. Since this moment is my "go-to" for focusing on good things, many times, I will watch our wedding video when feeling worried or anxious. God brought my wife and me there and gave us that moment. He delights in us and loves to give us good things. As I stop to reflect on God's love for me and how faithful He is to give us joyful and happy moments as well as carry and guide us through hard times, it makes it easy to rejoice.

> *The Spirit of the Lord is on me, because he has anointed me to proclaim the good news to the poor. He has sent me to proclaim freedom for the prisoners and recovery of sight for the blind. To set the oppressed free, to proclaim the year of the Lord's favor.*
>
> *Luke 4:18–19 NIV*

Jesus read these words of Isaiah in the synagogue in his hometown of Nazareth and then said:

> *Today this scripture is fulfilled in your hearing.*
>
> *Luke 4:21 NIV*

Turn to Jesus and ask for His help. This is why He was sent. Ask for His strength.

> *I can do all things through Him who strengthens me.*
>
> *Philippians 4:13 NASB2020*

We often hear Christians talk about the flesh and about the world and our struggles with them. But Paul tells us clearly in Ephesians that our struggle is not with flesh or with the world itself, but rather our struggle is with the devil and his schemes.

> *Put on the full armor of God, so that you can take your stand against the devil's schemes. For our struggle is not against flesh and blood, but*

> *against the rulers, against the authorities, against the powers of this dark world and against the spiritual forces of evil in the heavenly realms.*
>
> *Ephesians 6:11–12 NIV*

There are many thoughts and opinions on whether or not flesh is just our own sinful nature or if the devil is involved with all sin. My personal thoughts are that he is. Eve was flesh, and she did not sin until she was tempted. And again, Paul says above that our struggle is not against flesh but against the powers of the dark world, which leads me to believe that these powers are involved with all sin. And looking back to Chapter 4, we reviewed that the Bible defines sin in this way—

> *Everyone who sins breaks the law;*
> *in fact, sin is lawlessness.*
>
> *1 John 3:4 NIV*
>
> *If anyone, then, knows the good they ought*
> *to do and doesn't do it, it is sin for them.*
>
> *James 4:17 NIV*

And friends, you are not alone! Our enemy is ruthless and unrelenting. We see in Scripture that the Apostle Paul struggled as well.

> *I do not understand what I do. For what I want*
> *to do I do not do, but what I hate I do.*
>
> *Romans 7:15 NIV*

But then, Paul goes on to say—

And if I do what I do not want to do, I agree that the law is good. As it is, it is no longer I myself who do it, but it is sin living in me. For I know that good itself does not dwell in me, that is, in my sinful nature. For I have the desire to do what is good, but I cannot carry it out. For I do not do the good I want to do, but the evil I do not want to do—this I keep doing. Now if I do what I do not want to do, it is no longer I who do it, but it is sin living in me that does it.

So I find this law at work: Although I want to do good, evil is right there with me. For in my inner being I delight in God's law; but I see another law at work in me, waging war against the law of my mind and making me a prisoner of the law of sin at work within me. What a wretched man I am! Who will rescue me from this body that is subject to death? Thanks be to God, who delivers me through Jesus Christ our Lord!

So then, I myself in my mind am a slave to God's law, but in my sinful nature a slave to the law of sin.

Romans 7:16-25 NIV

Paul sees two separate entities at work within him, in conflict within him—a good nature and a sinful nature. But you can see that Paul identifies himself as the nature that is good. He acknowledges that the sinful nature is "right there with him." But it is no longer himself that does it but the sin living in him.

Now this is not meant to be taken as a license to just let the sinful nature take over. Not at all. "The devil made me do it" is not true. What is true is that the devil will entice you and tempt you. And if he is successful, he will then come around again and hit you with the double whammy of guilt and shame.

> *So I say, walk by the Spirit, and you will not gratify the desires of the flesh. For the flesh desires what is contrary to the Spirit, and the Spirit what is contrary to the flesh. They are in conflict with each other, so that you are not to do whatever you want.*
>
> Galatians 5:16–17 NIV

But understand friends, there are evil forces at work. They want the sinful nature to win the battle every time. And if it does, the evil one will use it against you.

In his book, *The Utter Relief of Holiness*, John Eldredge says this:

> *The greatest weapon you will ever have against the enemy is holiness. Warfare often works like a presidential election—they go through all of your old files. Satan is looking for anything he can find to use against you. He'll drudge up old sins, he'll create strongholds through ancient agreements, he'll exploit your wounds and your idolatries to ensnare you.*[24]

The less sin you have in your life, the less the devil will have to use against you. And, no, there are none of us without sin. But if you are faithful to confess your sin to God, ask for forgiveness, and truly repent, you know that you are truly forgiven and are right and righteous with God.

---

[24] Eldredge, John. *The Utter Relief of Holiness: How God's Goodness Frees Us From Everything That Plagues Us.* Thomas Nelson, 2003.

Let Us Pray

> *Rejoice always, pray continually, give thanks in all circumstances, for this is God's will for you in Christ Jesus.*
>
> *1 Thessalonians 5:16–18 NIV*

> *And the prayer offered in faith will make the sick person well; the Lord will raise them up. If they have sinned, they will be forgiven. Therefore, confess your sins to each other and pray for each other so that you may be healed. The prayer of a righteous person is powerful and effective.*
>
> *Elijah was a human being, even as we are. He prayed earnestly that it would not rain, and it did not rain on the land for three and a half years. Again he prayed, and the heavens gave rain, and the earth produced its crops.*
>
> *James 5:15–18 NIV*

Let's go back to the Book of 1 Kings to see what James is referring to here when he mentions Elijah.

> *And Elijah said to Ahab, "Go, eat and drink, for there is the sound of a heavy rain." So Ahab went off to eat and drink, but Elijah climbed to the top of Carmel, bent down to the ground and put his face between his knees.*
>
> *"Go and look toward the sea," he told his servant. And he went up and looked.*

> *"There is nothing there," he said.*
>
> *Seven times Elijah said, "Go back."*
>
> *The seventh time the servant reported, "A cloud as small as a man's hand is rising from the sea."*
>
> *So Elijah said, "Go and tell Ahab, 'Hitch up your chariot and go down before the rain stops you.'"*
>
> 1 Kings 18:41–44 NIV

James tells us that Elijah was a human, just like us. But he kept praying! He did not give up. We may not always see results the first time we pray. But we must not give up.

> *Let us not become weary in doing good, for at the proper time we will reap a harvest if we do not give up.*
>
> Galatians 6:9 NIV

Possession vs. Oppression

Most of the examples we see in the New Testament are cases of demonic possession—that is, a demon is actually dwelling in an individual and controlling them. We see no examples of believers in the New Testament being possessed by a demon. We do see examples of non-believers being possessed, and these are the spirits that we see Jesus and the disciples driving out. The fact that we see no examples in Scripture of a believer being possessed or instruction for driving demons out of a believer leads me to believe that a believer cannot be possessed by a demon. In fact, Scripture tells us that Christ now dwells in believers—

*I have been crucified with Christ and I no
longer live, but Christ lives in me.*

Galatians 2:20 NIV

*To them God has chosen to make known among
the Gentiles the glorious riches of this mystery,
which is Christ in you, the hope of glory.*

Colossians 1:27 NIV

*I pray that out of his glorious riches he may strengthen
you with power through his Spirit in your inner being,
so that Christ may dwell in your hearts through faith.*

Ephesians 3:16–17 NIV

*Examine yourselves to see whether you are in
the faith; Do you not realize that Christ Jesus is
in you—unless, of course, you fail the test?*

2 Corinthians 13:5 NIV

And Jesus Himself tells us this as well—
*I have given them the glory that you gave me, that
they may be one as we are one—I in them, and you
in me—so that they may be brought to complete
unity. Then the world will know that you sent me
and have loved them even as you have loved me.*

John 17:22–23 NIV

Remain in me, as I also remain in you.

John 15:4 NIV

We can see clearly from Scripture that as believers, Jesus lives in us. We may not always feel His presence, and at times may even have doubts, but these feelings and doubts are lies from Satan himself.

Jesus also reveals something very important to us in Matthew 12:

> *When an impure spirit comes out of a person, it goes through arid places seeking rest and does not find it. Then it says, 'I will return to the house I left.' When it arrives, it finds the house unoccupied, swept clean, and put in order. Then it goes and takes with it seven other spirits more wicked than itself, and they go in and live there. And the condition of that person is worse than the first. That is how it will be with this wicked generation.*
>
> Matthew 12:43–45 NIV

I believe what Jesus is telling us is this—an *unoccupied* house is open to evil spirits to come in and live there. As believers, Jesus lives in us. We are no longer unoccupied. The evil spirits can no longer come in, as Jesus has all authority over everything, including Satan and his evil spirits.

> *You, dear children, are from God and have overcome them, because the one who is in you is greater than the one who is in the world.*
>
> 1 John 4:4 NIV

As Christians, we cannot be possessed by a demon. But we can be oppressed and influenced by them. As believers, we deal with spiritual oppression rather than possession. Our flesh or sinful nature is not possession, as we still have control. We still have a choice. But we must always strive to make the right choice.

But demonic possession is certainly possible for non-believers. We can see from Paul's example in Acts that we can, as believers, through the power of the Holy Spirit and, in the name and the authority of Jesus Christ, cast demons out of people who are possessed. We will get into that more later in Chapter 17, but for now, I want us to focus on spiritual oppression.

Spiritual Oppression

While Scripture does not mention a believer being possessed, there are scriptures that warn believers of demonic oppression.

For our struggle is not against flesh and blood, but against the rulers, against the authorities, against the powers of this dark world and against the spiritual forces of evil in the heavenly realms.

Ephesians 6:13 NIV

Be alert and of sober mind. Your enemy the devil prowls around like a roaring lion looking for someone to devour. Resist him, standing firm in the faith, because you know that the family of believers throughout the world is undergoing the same kind of suffering.

1 Peter 5:8–9 NIV

Submit yourselves then, to God. Resist the devil, and he will flee from you.

James 4:7 NIV

Both Peter and James tell us to resist the devil. These letters were written to believers. Peter tells us to stand firm in the faith, and James tells us to submit ourselves to God. Standing firm in the faith and submitting ourselves to God play a huge part in resisting the devil. James is very direct—submit to God, resist the devil, and he will flee from you. Well, it's time to let you in on a little secret—the previous Chapters 3 through 9 tell us how to submit ourselves to God and stand firm in the faith. We have covered union with God, sin, repentance, forgiveness, faith, trust, prayer, fasting, our authority, and the Armor of God, all of which will significantly reduce the impact of spiritual attacks in our lives.

Friends, God should always be our focus. We should not go out looking for a fight. But at times, in addition to prayer, it is also helpful to directly rebuke these evil spirits.

Prayer

Daily prayer is of the utmost importance. When it comes to spiritual attack, think of prayer as a pre-emptive attack strategy. John Eldredge has a great daily prayer which can be found here:

https://wildatheart.org/prayer/daily-prayer-john

It's about 10 minutes long. I have modified it a bit to reflect my life and situation, but it is a great prayer with much scriptural context.

And I will add here, before we go any further, that the chapters on preparing yourself are so important. If there is any unconfessed sin or unforgiveness in your heart, please take the time to take care of that now.

When I am really feeling under attack, many times, I will get down on my knees and pray. I feel this submission really helps. When I am rebuking, however, I stand tall to rebuke! Also, when possible, I will pray and rebuke out loud. Now, depending on your situation or location, this may not always be possible.

We know from Chapter 9 that Satan does not have the same power as God. God is omnipotent and omnipresent. Satan is not. God knows our thoughts. Satan does not. However, Satan can study us and do his best to discern our thoughts. Scripture tells us:

Satan himself masquerades as an angel of light.

2 Corinthians 11:14 NIV

So, there are times that I want to make sure that Satan does not hear my prayers. I will pray silently, as I know that God will hear me. But since Satan is not omnipotent and omnipresent, I always try to speak rebukes out loud.

There are also times when I may be praying for someone else who is under attack. And those people may not always be in my location. In fact, they may be hundreds or even thousands of miles from me. God will hear and receive those prayers. But what about a rebuke? If the devil is not omnipresent and can't hear my silent prayers, how can I effectively rebuke attacks either from a distance or through silent prayer? Well, while the devil is not omnipresent, God is! So, for these rebukes, I call on the Holy Spirit, who is omnipotent and omnipresent—all-powerful and everywhere all the time.

Since we covered prayer and fasting in Chapter 6, let's move on to rebuke.

Rebuke

Rebuke is different from prayer. It is still spiritual, but instead of praying to God, you are addressing a deceiving spirit directly.

In the Book of Matthew, Jesus tells us:

> *But if it is by the Spirit of God that I drive out demons, then the kingdom of God has come upon you.*
>
> *Or again, how can anyone enter a strong man's house and carry off his possessions unless he first ties up the strong man? Then he can plunder his house.*
>
> *Matthew 12:28–29 NIV*

Immediately after Jesus speaks of driving out demons, He uses a parable. The reference here would be that the demon is the strong man, and he must be tied up.

In the Book of Ecclesiastes, Solomon says this:

> *A cord of three strands is not quickly broken.*
>
> *Ecclesiastes 4:12 NIV*

And in 2 Corinthians, Paul tells us this:

> *For though we live in the world, we do not wage war as the world does. The weapons we fight with are not weapons of the world. On the contrary, they have divine power to demolish strongholds. We demolish arguments and every pretension that sets itself up against the knowledge of God, and we take captive every thought and make it obedient to Christ.*
>
> *2 Corinthians 10:3–5 NIV*

In Philippians, Paul also tells us this:

Therefore God exalted him to the highest place and gave him the name that is above every name, that at the name of Jesus every knee should bow, in heaven and on earth and under the earth, and every tongue acknowledge that Jesus Christ is Lord, to the glory of God the Father.

Philippians 2:9–11 NIV

And from the Book of Isaiah:

"No weapon formed against you will prevail, and you will refute every tongue that accuses you. This is the heritage of the servants of the LORD, and this is their vindication from me," declares the LORD.

Isaiah 54:17 NIV

And remember, God created us in His image, and He blesses us:

So God created mankind in his own image, in the image of God he created them, male and female he created them. God blessed them and said to them, "Be fruitful and increase in number; fill the earth and subdue it."

Genesis 1:27–28 NIV

And there is also a place prepared for the evil one:

Then he will say to those on his left, "Depart from me, you who are cursed, into the eternal fire prepared for the devil and his angels."

Matthew 25:41 NIV

Yes, we do live in the world, but our weapons are not of this world, as this is a spiritual battle. These weapons do have the power to demolish *every* stronghold the devil may have. We also see that the enemy's main objective is to separate us from the knowledge of God, to get us to take our eyes off Him and focus on the trouble around us. How easily he can distract us if we let him! But most of the time, the battle is in our heads. We use the Word of God to demolish the stronghold, get it out of our heads, and get our thoughts back on Jesus.

Remember, from Chapter 8, our offensive weapon from the Armor of God is the Word of God. Use Scripture whenever you can in rebuke. These last several scriptures are really good ones to memorize, so they are readily available to you when you need them. And you may have noticed that I have referenced many verses repeatedly throughout this book—also good ones to memorize.

I believe our best example of rebuke comes from Jesus Himself. Let's take another look at that from the Book of Matthew.

> *The tempter came to him and said, "If you are the Son of God, tell these stones to become bread."*
>
> *Jesus answered, "It is written: 'Man shall not live on bread alone, but on every word that comes from the mouth of God.'"*
>
> Matthew 4:3-4 NIV

In this and the next two temptations, Jesus says, "It is written," and then He cites specific Scripture. I don't think there is a better way to do it than the example set for us by Jesus. And I also need to point out here that when tempted, Jesus rebuked Satan with Scripture, but He also didn't do what

He was being tempted to do. Friends, Scripture will help us to rebuke Satan. But we also must choose not to sin. God gives us free will, and that is where the devil will attack us. That is part of resisting the devil. We must make the choice not to sin.

Paul, when describing the Armor of God, says that the Sword of the Spirit is the Word of God. I don't believe we have to be this specific with Scripture in our prayers, as God wants to hear from our hearts! But in our rebukes, let's follow the example of Jesus.

In the next few chapters, we will review some examples of prayer and rebuke for different situations.

CHAPTER 11

How We Fight Fear

Fear can be a good thing at certain times. In fact, fear can save your life. It triggers our fight-or-flight reaction. When attacked, fear can trigger you to fight. When a tornado is heading your way, fear can lead you to seek immediate shelter. But fear is also one of the devil's most powerful weapons. When the fear is in your head, the results can be damaging. It can paralyze you and make you ineffective. Or, on the other extreme, it can lead you to do things that may harm you or harm others. But 2 Timothy reminds us that we do not have a spirit of fear:

> *For the Spirit God gave us does not make us timid, but gives us power, love and self-discipline.*
>
> *2 Timothy 1:7 NIV*

Let's include that in our prayers and rebuke for fear, along with some other helpful verses on fear as well:

> *But now, this is what the LORD says—he who created you, Jacob, he who formed you, Israel:*

> *"Do not fear, for I have redeemed you; I have summoned you by name; you are mine."*
>
> Isaiah 43:1 NIV

> *Have I not commanded you? Be strong and courageous. Do not be afraid; do not be discouraged, for the LORD your God will be with you wherever you go.*
>
> Joshua 1:9 NIV

> *Even though I walk through the darkest valley, I will fear no evil, for you are with me; your rod and your staff, they comfort me.*
>
> Psalm 23:4 NIV

> *Peace I leave with you; my peace I give you. I do not give to you as the world gives. Do not let your hearts be troubled, and do not be afraid.*
>
> John 14:27 NIV

We can build a prayer for overcoming fear using the Word of God. I have used the example scriptures I just shared. You can choose to use some of these scriptures, all of these scriptures, or use different scriptures to add to these or to create your own.

Here's an example:

Heavenly Father, Lord Jesus, Holy Spirit—

I come to you today seeking union with you, God. I praise You for who You are—God Almighty! The creator of the heavens and the earth. The creator of me. I was created in Your image, and You bless me (Genesis 1:27–28). You created my inmost being. You knit me together in my mother's womb, and I am fearfully and wonderfully made. I know that Your works are wonderful (Psalm 139:13–14).

Heavenly Father, Lord Jesus, Holy Spirit, I am under attack. I ask You for Your guidance and strength. Fill me with Your Holy Spirit, God, and give me Your strength to resist, rebuke, and fight these attacks.

Lord Jesus, I am fearful. But the Spirit You gave me is not a spirit of fear, but rather gives me power, love, and self-discipline (2 Timothy 1:7). Holy Spirit, fill me today. You are not fear. You are power, love, and self-discipline to conquer fear. I release all my fear of (blank) to You, God. (Describe the situation that you are afraid of. If you don't know why you are afraid, just say fear. Jesus knows!)

Almighty God, You created me and formed me. You have redeemed me and summoned me by name, and I am Yours. I will not be afraid (Isaiah 43:1).

Almighty God, You are with me wherever I go. Help me to be strong and courageous. Help me not to be afraid. I need the help that only You can give me, God (Joshua 1:9).

Almighty God, I am in a dark place, but I know You are with me. You are with me, so I will not fear evil. Fill me with Your comfort God (Psalm 23:4).

Lord Jesus, You give me Your peace, and I receive it with thanks. Help my heart not to be troubled, and help me not to be afraid. Fill me with Your peace Jesus (John 14:27).

Almighty God, may all this be accomplished now by You and through the mighty name of my Lord and Savior, Jesus Christ. I give You all glory, honor, thanks, and praise.

I love You, I trust You, and I worship You.

In Jesus' name, I pray,

Amen.

We can create a powerful rebuke using the same scripture verses. Again, you can choose to use some of these scriptures, all of these scriptures, or use different scriptures to add to these or create your own rebuke. To start the rebuke, I suggest declaring who we are in Christ. It's not only a good reminder for the devil but a good reminder for us when we are being attacked. If possible, I suggest you stand and speak rebukes out loud:

God created me and formed me in His image and blesses me, for it is written, *"So God created mankind in his own image, in the image of God he created them; male and female he created them. God blessed them and said to them, 'Be fruitful and increase in number; fill the earth and subdue it'"* (Genesis 1:27-28 NIV).

God created me and knows me, and I am wonderfully made, for it is written, *"For you created my inmost being; you knit me together in my mother's womb. I praise you because I am fearfully and wonderfully made; your works are wonderful, I know that full well"* (Psalm 139:13-14 NIV).

I believe Jesus Christ is the Son of God. He is my Lord and Savior. I am a child of God, and I belong to Him, for it is written, "*Yet to all who did receive him, to those who believed in his name, he gave the right to become children of God*" (John 1:12 NIV).

In the name and in the authority of my Lord and Savior Jesus Christ, and by and through the Holy Spirit, I now use the three-strand cord of God from Ecclesiastes to bind up all spirits of fear that are attacking me now, for it is written, "*A cord of three strands is not quickly broken*" (Ecclesiastes 4:12 NIV).

In the name and in the authority of my Lord and Savior Jesus Christ, I command you bound, tied up, and rendered useless, for it is written, "*How can anyone enter a strong man's house and carry off his possessions unless he first ties up the strong man? Then he can plunder his house*" (Matthew 12:29 NIV).

All authority in heaven and on earth has been given to Jesus, for Jesus said of Himself, and it is written, "*All authority in heaven and on earth has been given to me*" (Matthew 28:18 NIV).

The name of Jesus is above all names, for it is written, "*Therefore God exalted him to the highest place and gave him the name that is above every name, that at the name of Jesus every knee should bow, in heaven and on earth and under the earth, and every tongue acknowledge that Jesus Christ is Lord, to the glory of God the Father*" (Philippians 2:9–11 NIV).

I command all spirits of fear tied up and bound in the name and in the authority of my Lord and Savior, Jesus Christ, and you must submit to Him and His authority.

The Spirit of God is in me, and the Holy Spirit does not make me fearful. The Holy Spirit gives me power, love, and self-discipline, for it is written, *"For the Spirit God gave us does not make us timid, but gives us power, love and self-discipline"* (2 Timothy 1:7 NIV).

I am not afraid because God has redeemed me and called me by name, and I belong to Him, for it is written, *"But now, this is what the LORD says—he who created you, Jacob, he who formed you, Israel: Do not fear, for I have redeemed you; I have summoned you by name; you are mine"* (Isaiah 43:1 NIV).

I am not afraid, and I am not discouraged because God is with me wherever I go. I am strong and courageous, for it is written, *"Have I not commanded you? Be strong and courageous. Do not be afraid; do not be discouraged, for the LORD your God will be with you wherever you go"* (Joshua 1:9 NIV).

I may be in a dark place, but I am not afraid because God is with me and gives me comfort, for it is written, *"Even though I walk through the darkest valley, I will fear no evil, for you are with me; your rod and your staff, they comfort me"* (Psalm 23:4 NIV). I claim the peace of Jesus in my life and in my mind, and I am not afraid.

In the name and in the authority of my Lord and Savior Jesus Christ, and by and through the Holy Spirit, I declare all strongholds of fear demolished, for it is written, *"For though we live in the world, we do not wage war as the world does. The weapons we fight with are not the weapons of the world. On the contrary, they have divine power to demolish strongholds"* (2 Corinthians 10:4 NIV).

In the name and in the authority of my Lord and Savior Jesus Christ, and by and through the Holy Spirit, I now command all spirits of fear to leave me. All spirits of fear, all backups and replacements, all weapons and devices, for it is written, *"'No weapon forged against you will prevail, and you will refute every tongue that accuses you. This is the heritage of the servants of the LORD, and this is their vindication from me,'* declares the LORD" (Isaiah 54:17 NIV).

In the name and in the authority of my Lord and Savior Jesus Christ, I now banish all spirits of fear from me and command you bound to the feet of Jesus for judgment with the three-strand cord of God, for it is written, *"Depart from me, you who are cursed, into the eternal fire prepared for the devil and his angels"* (Matthew 25:41 NIV).

Now we can switch back to prayer.

Almighty God, may all this be accomplished now by You and through the mighty name of my Lord and Savior, Jesus Christ. I give You all glory, honor, thanks, and praise. I love You, I trust You, and I worship You. Jesus, I ask this in Your name,

Amen.

Fear can be a good thing at times. But it can also paralyze us and make us ineffective. Don't let the devil hold you back with fear from what God has called you to do.

Worry and anxiety are similar to fear, but there are some differences. We'll explore them both in the next chapter.

CHAPTER 12

How We Fight Worry and Anxiety

Two other powerful weapons of the devil are worry and anxiety. Worry and anxiety are similar to, but different than, fear. In her blog, Registered Clinical Counsellor Sharon Selby puts it this way:

> *When we are trying to tell the difference between worry, anxiety, or fear, it is often best to think of it as a continuum. Worry is at the beginning of the scale, anxiety is in the middle, and fear/panic is at the end.*[25]

As is with fear, worry and anxiety can hinder us as well, making us ineffective. Worrying can make us overthink things and give us *analysis paralysis*. When worry escalates to anxiety, anxiety can cause us to obsess over things and perhaps act impulsively. And yes, I do speak from personal experience.

Another difference between fear, worry, and anxiety is that, in many cases, fear represents an immediate threat. Worry and anxiety are often "what-if" scenarios that play out in our minds. Things that may happen in the future.

---

[25] Selby, S. 2018. *What Is the Difference Between Sorry and Anxiety or Fear?* Retrieved from https://www.sharonselby.com/anxiety/what-is-the-difference-between-worry-anxiety-and-fear

And something that may help ease your worried minds? Nearly all the things we worry about never happen. *Never happen.* In a Penn State University study, Lucas LaFreniere and Michelle Newman found that, on average, 91.39 % of worries don't come true.[26] That means less than 9% of worries actually come true. Yet how much time and mental cycles do we spend on worry? No wonder it is part of the devil's arsenal!

Let's look at some Scripture about worry and anxiety.

*Therefore do not worry about tomorrow,
for tomorrow will worry about itself. Each
day has enough trouble of its own.*

Matthew 6:34 NIV

*Peace I leave with you; my peace I give you. I
do not give to you as the world gives. Do not let
your hearts be troubled, and do not be afraid.*

John 14:27 NIV

Cast all your anxiety on him, because he cares for you.

1 Peter 5:7 NIV

*Cast all your cares on the LORD, and he will sustain
you; he will never let the righteous be shaken.*

Psalm 55:22 NIV

Now, as we did before, let's turn these scriptures (or scriptures of your own choosing) into a prayer.

Heavenly Father, Lord Jesus, Holy Spirit—

---

[26] LaFreniere, L. Newman, M. 2019. Retrieved from https://www.sciencedirect.com/science/article/abs/pii/S0005789419300826#

I come to you today seeking union with you, God. I praise you for who you are—God Almighty! The creator of the heavens and the earth. The creator of me. I was created in your image, and you bless me (Genesis 1:27-28). You created my inmost being. You knit me together in my mother's womb, and I am fearfully and wonderfully made. I know that your works are wonderful (Psalm 139:13-14).

Heavenly Father, Lord Jesus, Holy Spirit, I am under attack. I ask You for your guidance and strength. Fill me with Your Holy Spirit, God, and give me Your strength to resist, rebuke, and fight these attacks.

Lord Jesus, I am worried. I am anxious. But the Spirit You gave me is not a spirit of worry, but rather gives me power, love, and self-discipline (2 Timothy 1:7). Holy Spirit, fill me today. You are not about worry. You are power, love, and self-discipline to conquer worry. I release all my worry about (blank) to You, God. (Describe the situation or situations that you are worried about. And again, sometimes we just feel anxious and don't know why. Just tell Jesus about it. Release it to Him.)

Lord Jesus, help me not to worry about (blank) that is coming up tomorrow (or later today, or next week, next month, whenever). Jesus, I give this to You. I release this to You, God (Matthew 6:34).

Lord Jesus, You give me Your peace, and I receive it with thanks. Fill me with Your peace Jesus, so that my heart will not be troubled with worry (John 14:27).

Jesus, I give this all to You. I know that You love me and care for me (1 Peter 5:7).

Jesus, sustain me as I release this worry to You. Let me not be shaken (Psalm 55:22).

Almighty God, may all this be accomplished now by You and through the mighty name of my Lord and Savior, Jesus Christ. I give You all glory, honor, thanks, and praise.

I love You, I trust You, and I worship You.

In Jesus' name, I pray,

Amen.

And again, we can create a powerful rebuke for worry and anxiety using these same scriptures or scriptures of your choosing. I suggest starting with declaring who we are in Christ and standing and speaking this aloud if possible.

God created me and formed me in His image and blesses me, for it is written, "*So God created mankind in his own image, in the image of God he created them; male and female he created them. God blessed them and said to them, 'Be fruitful and increase in number; fill the earth and subdue it'*" (Genesis 1:27–28 NIV).

God created me and knows me, and I am wonderfully made, for it is written, "*For you created my inmost being; you knit me together in my mother's womb. I praise you because I am fearfully and wonderfully made; your works are wonderful, I know that full well*" (Psalm 139:13–14 NIV).

I believe Jesus Christ is the Son of God. He is my Lord and Savior. I am a child of God, and I belong to Him, for it is written, "*Yet to all who did receive him, to those who believed in his name, he gave the right to become children of God"* (John 1:12 NIV).

In the name and in the authority of my Lord and Savior Jesus Christ, and by and through the Holy Spirit, I now use the three-strand cord of God from Ecclesiastes to bind up all spirits of worry and anxiety that are attacking me now, for it is written, *"A cord of three strands is not quickly broken"* (Ecclesiastes 4:12 NIV).

In the name and in the authority of my Lord and Savior Jesus Christ, I command you bound, tied up, and rendered useless, for it is written, *"How can anyone enter a strong man's house and carry off his possessions unless he first ties up the strong man? Then he can plunder his house"* (Matthew 12:29 NIV).

All authority in heaven and on earth has been given to Jesus, for Jesus said of Himself, and it is written, *"All authority in heaven and on earth has been given to me"* (Matthew 28:18 NIV).

The name of Jesus is above all names, for it is written, *"Therefore God exalted him to the highest place and gave him the name that is above every name, that at the name of Jesus every knee should bow, in heaven and on earth and under the earth, and every tongue acknowledge that Jesus Christ is Lord, to the glory of God the Father"* (Philippians 2:9–11 NIV). I command all spirits of worry and anxiety tied up and bound in the name and in the authority of my Lord and Savior, Jesus Christ, and you must submit to Him and His authority.

The Spirit of God is in me, and the Holy Spirit does not make me worried or anxious. The Holy Spirit gives me power, love, and self-discipline, for it is written, *"For the Spirit God gave us does not make us timid, but gives us power, love and self-discipline"* (2 Timothy 1:7 NIV).

I do not worry about things to come because the Holy Spirit is in me, for it is written, "*Therefore do not worry about tomorrow, for tomorrow will worry about itself. Each day has enough trouble of its own*" (Matthew 6:34 NIV).

My heart is not troubled, and I am not worried because I have the peace of Jesus, for it is written, "*Peace I leave with you; my peace I give you. I do not give to you as the world gives. Do not let your hearts be troubled, and do not be afraid*" (John 14:27 NIV).

I have cast all my worries and anxieties on God because He cares for me, for it is written, "*Cast all your anxiety on him, because he cares for you*" (1 Peter 5:7 NIV).

And because I have given all my cares to God, He is sustaining me, and I will not be shaken, for it is written, "*Cast all your cares on the LORD, and he will sustain you; he will never let the righteous be shaken*" (Psalm 55:22 NIV).

In the name and in the authority of my Lord and Savior Jesus Christ, and by and through the Holy Spirit, I declare all strongholds of worry and anxiety demolished, for it is written, "*For though we live in the world, we do not wage war as the world does. The weapons we fight with are not the weapons of the world. On the contrary, they have divine power to demolish strongholds*" (2 Corinthians 10:4 NIV).

In the name and in the authority of my Lord and Savior Jesus Christ and by and through the Holy Spirit, I now command all spirits of worry and anxiety to leave me. All spirits of worry and anxiety, all backups and replacements, all weapons and devices, for it is written, "'*No weapon forged against you will prevail, and you will refute every tongue that accuses you. This is the heritage of the servants of the LORD, and this is their vindication from me,' declares the LORD*" (Isaiah 54:17 NIV).

In the name and in the authority of my Lord and Savior Jesus Christ, I now banish all spirits of worry and anxiety from me and command you bound to the feet of Jesus for judgment with the three-strand cord of God, for it is written, "*Depart from me, you who are cursed, into the eternal fire prepared for the devil and his angels*" (Matthew 25:41 NIV).

Once again, let's switch back to prayer.

Almighty God, may all this be accomplished now by You and through the mighty name of my Lord and Savior, Jesus Christ. I give You all glory, honor, thanks, and praise. I love You, I trust You, and I worship You. Jesus, I ask this in Your name,

Amen.

Take comfort in knowing that nearly everything we worry about will never happen. And if it does happen, we are not alone. Jesus is always right there with us. But at times, we do feel as if we are alone. Let's look at that next.

CHAPTER 13

How We Fight
Abandonment and Loneliness

Fear of abandonment is recognized by psychologists, and it often has negative impacts on our relationships. In an article written on fear of abandonment, Licensed Christian Counselor Erik Mildes says this:

> *Do you feel unable to focus on your relationship without being consumed with fear that your partner will leave you? Do you expect that things won't last, but you feel compelled to test that theory by pushing your partner away or controlling them? Or, do you become clingy and needy because you desperately want to keep this person in your life? If any of these behaviors sound like you, you may be suffering from what psychologists call fear of abandonment, which means that you are afraid of being rejected and alone. You try to cope with your fear in ways that interfere with your relationships—or make potential relationships impossible.*
>
> *If you have a fear of abandonment, this probably affects your behavior in ways that you may not even realize. You don't have to be stuck in this pattern, though. It*

is possible to overcome your abandonment issues and have healthy relationships with people in your life.[27]

Mr. Mildes goes on to list five ways to help overcome a fear of abandonment. You can read the full article here:

https://seattlechristiancounseling.com/ articles/5-practical-steps-to-overcome-your-fear-of-abandonment

I call out feelings of abandonment specifically, again, because of personal experience. It is something that I have struggled with from time to time, and yes, it does negatively impact my relationships, especially with my wife. The time spent apart from my wife while caring for my mother has been difficult for me. This much time apart can be a challenge for any relationship, and my feelings of loneliness and abandonment, coupled with my behavior it has led to at times, have definitely had a negative impact. I thank my wife and God for her patience, grace, understanding, and forgiveness. But I have found prayer, meditation, and keeping my focus on the present, not going back to should-haves of the past or what-ifs of the future, does help tremendously. Dwelling in the past is pointless. You cannot change it. You can look to the past to learn from it and grow from it, but don't let yourself get stuck there. Looking to the future can be good to help you plan for it, which can actually reduce worry. But dwelling in the future isn't good either. You are best to stay in the present. Your own actions, in the present, are really the only thing you have any control over.

---

[27] Mildes, E. 2020. *5 Practical Steps to Overcome Your Fear of Abandonment*. Retrieved from https://seattlechristiancounseling.com/articles/ 5-practical-steps-to-overcome-your-fear-of-abandonment

Let's look at some Scripture that is helpful when you are feeling lonely or abandoned:

> *The LORD himself goes before you and will be with you; he will never leave you nor forsake you. Do not be afraid, do not be discouraged.*
>
> *Deuteronomy 31:8 NIV*
>
> *The LORD replied, "My Presence will go with you, and I will give you rest."*
>
> *Exodus 33:14 NIV*
>
> *For I am convinced that neither death nor life, neither angels nor demons, neither present nor the future, nor any powers, neither height nor depth, nor anything else in creation, will be able to separate us from the love of God that is in Christ Jesus our Lord.*
>
> *Romans 8:38–39 NIV*
>
> *And surely I am with you always, to the very end of the age.*
>
> *Matthew 28:20 NIV*

Let's build another prayer, this time for abandonment and loneliness. You can use some or all of these verses or verses of your own choosing.

Heavenly Father, Lord Jesus, Holy Spirit—

I come to you today seeking union with You, God. I praise You for who You are—God Almighty! The creator of the heavens and the earth. The creator of me. I was created in Your image, and You bless me (Genesis

1:27–28). You created my inmost being. You knit me together in my mother's womb, and I am fearfully and wonderfully made. I know that Your works are wonderful (Psalm 139:13–14).

Heavenly Father, Lord Jesus, Holy Spirit, I am under attack. I ask You for Your guidance and strength. Fill me with Your Holy Spirit, God, and give me Your strength to resist, rebuke, and fight these attacks.

Lord Jesus, I am feeling lonely and abandoned. But the Spirit You give me gives me power, love, and self-discipline (2 Timothy 1:7). Holy Spirit, fill me today. You are always with me. You are power, love, and self-discipline to conquer loneliness. I release all my fear of abandonment and loneliness to You, God. (Describe the situation that is making you feel lonely or abandoned.)

God, You go before me, and You are with me. I know You will never leave me, and You will never forsake me (Deuteronomy 31:8).

Help me today to feel Your presence with me, God, and give me rest (Exodus 33:14).

God, nothing can separate me from Your love. Jesus, let me feel Your love surround me today (Romans 8:38–39).

Jesus, thank You for always being with me. Let me feel Your presence with me today, Jesus (Matthew 28:20).

I release all my feelings of loneliness and abandonment to You, Jesus.

Almighty God, may all this be accomplished now by You and through the mighty name of my Lord and Savior, Jesus Christ. I give You all glory, honor, thanks, and praise.

I love You, I trust You, and I worship You.

In Jesus' name, I pray,

Amen.

And now, let's rebuke deceitful spirits of loneliness and abandonment. Again, you can use some or all these verses if you'd like or use verses of your own choosing.

God created me and formed me in His image and blesses me, for it is written, "*So God created mankind in his own image, in the image of God he created them; male and female he created them. God blessed them and said to them, 'Be fruitful and increase in number; fill the earth and subdue it'*" (Genesis 1:27–28 NIV).

God created me and knows me, and I am wonderfully made, for it is written, "*For you created my inmost being; you knit me together in my mother's womb. I praise you because I am fearfully and wonderfully made; your works are wonderful, I know that full well*" (Psalm 139:13–14 NIV).

I believe Jesus Christ is the Son of God. He is my Lord and Savior. I am a child of God, and I belong to Him, for it is written, "*Yet to all who did receive him, to those who believed in his name, he gave the right to become children of God*" (John 1:12 NIV).

In the name and in the authority of my Lord and Savior Jesus Christ, and by and through the Holy Spirit, I now use the three-strand cord of God from Ecclesiastes to bind up all spirits of abandonment and loneliness that are attacking me now, for it is written, "*A cord of three strands is not quickly broken*" (Ecclesiastes 4:12 NIV).

In the name and in the authority of my Lord and Savior Jesus Christ, I command you bound, tied up, and rendered useless, for it is written, "*How can anyone enter a strong man's house and carry off his possessions unless he first ties up the strong man? Then he can plunder his house*" (Matthew 12:29 NIV).

All authority in heaven and on earth has been given to Jesus, for Jesus said of Himself, and it is written, "*All authority in heaven and on earth has been given to me*" (Matthew 28:18 NIV).

The name of Jesus is above all names, for it is written, "*Therefore God exalted him to the highest place and gave him the name that is above every name, that at the name of Jesus every knee should bow, in heaven and on earth and under the earth, and every tongue acknowledge that Jesus Christ is Lord, to the glory of God the Father*" (Philippians 2:9–11 NIV).

I command all spirits of abandonment and loneliness tied up and bound in the name and in the authority of my Lord and Savior, Jesus Christ, and you must submit to Him and His authority.

The Spirit of God is in me, and the Holy Spirit does not make me fearful of abandonment. The Holy Spirit gives me power, love, and self-discipline, for it is written, "*For the Spirit God gave us does not make us timid, but gives us power, love and self-discipline*" (2 Timothy 1:7 NIV).

I am not abandoned because God is with me, for it is written, "*The LORD himself goes before you and will be with you; he will never leave you nor forsake you. Do not be afraid, do not be discouraged*" (Deuteronomy 31:8 NIV).

I am not abandoned because God is with me and gives me rest, for it is written, "*The LORD replied, 'My Presence will go with you, and I will give you rest'*" (Exodus 33:14 NIV).

You cannot separate me from God's love for me, for it is written, "*For I am convinced that neither death nor life, neither angels nor demons, neither present nor the future, nor any powers, neither height nor depth, nor anything else in creation, will be able to separate us from the love of God that is in Christ Jesus our Lord*" (Romans 8:38–39 NIV).

Jesus Himself is with me, for He said, and it is written, "*And surely I am with you always, to the very end of the age*" (Matthew 28:20 NIV).

In the name and in the authority of my Lord and Savior Jesus Christ, and by and through the Holy Spirit, I declare all strongholds of abandonment and loneliness demolished, for it is written, "*For though we live in the world, we do not wage war as the world does. The weapons we fight with are not the weapons of the world. On the contrary, they have divine power to demolish strongholds*" (2 Corinthians 10:4 NIV).

In the name and in the authority of my Lord and Savior Jesus Christ and by and through the Holy Spirit, I now command all spirits of abandonment and loneliness to leave me. All spirits of abandonment and loneliness, all backups and replacements, all weapons and devices, for it is written, "'*No weapon forged against you will prevail, and you will refute every tongue that accuses you. This is the heritage of the servants of the LORD, and this is their vindication from me,*' declares the LORD" (Isaiah 54:17 NIV).

In the name and in the authority of my Lord and Savior Jesus Christ, I now banish all spirits of abandonment and loneliness from me and command you bound to the feet of Jesus for judgment with the three-strand cord of God, for it is written, "*Depart from me, you who are cursed, into the eternal fire prepared for the devil and his angels*" (Matthew 25:41 NIV).

Once again, let's switch back to prayer.

Almighty God, may all this be accomplished now by You and through the mighty name of my Lord and Savior, Jesus Christ. I give You all glory, honor, thanks, and praise. I love You, I trust You, and I worship You. Jesus, I ask this in Your name,

Amen.

Remember, friends—we are never alone. Don't let the devil deceive you. Don't make this agreement with him.

At times, the storm going on around us may make us feel hopeless. This is from the devil as well. Let's go there next.

CHAPTER 14

How We Fight
Hopelessness and Despair

Hopelessness and despair can be difficult for many of us at times. This is where faith really comes into play. If you are dealing with this, I encourage you to go back and review Chapter 5, specifically the sections on faith, trust, and agreements. Faith calls us to look back and recall how faithful God has been to us. How He has delivered us. It can be easy to focus on the storm around us, especially when that is what the devil is feeding us. I myself have to do this often and look back at just how faithful God has been to deliver me out of whatever mess I find myself in. And no, it is usually not in my timing. Most times, I have to wait. Break any agreements you have made with a situation that you feel is hopeless.

> *You intended to harm me, but God intended it for good to accomplish what is now being done.*
>
> *Genesis 50:20 NIV*

Joseph had to wait. His brothers sold him into slavery. This was after they had contemplated killing him! He was sold as a slave to Potiphar, who was one of Pharaoh's officials. The Bible is not clear on how long Joseph was a slave to Potiphar, but God was with him and blessed him there, and Potiphar put Joseph in charge of his house. But Potiphar's wife tried to sleep with Joseph. She tried many times. One day when she tried, she caught him by his cloak. When he refused and ran from her, she held onto his cloak. She then took the cloak to her husband and accused Joseph of trying to rape her! Potiphar had Joseph thrown into prison.

We don't know how long Joseph was in prison, but while in prison, he met the cupbearer and the baker for Pharoah. Both men had dreams one night, and through God, Joseph was able to interpret their dreams. The cupbearer was reinstated, and the baker was impaled. And although Joseph had asked the cupbearer to mention this to Pharoah to help get Joseph out of prison, the cupbearer forgot Joseph until two years later. We don't know exactly how long Joseph was a slave to Potiphar, and we don't know how long he was in prison before interpreting the dream of the cupbearer, but we do know that two years passed before the cupbearer mentioned this to Pharoah. Then, Joseph was able to interpret a dream for Pharoah, and Pharoah put Joseph in charge of all of Egypt.

God did deliver Joseph. And Joseph remained faithful to God and righteous during his time as a slave and during his time in prison. God blessed him while he was with Potiphar, and God blessed him while he was in prison. But God didn't deliver Joseph from prison for over two years.

Years later, when his brothers came to Egypt, Joseph saved them. The same brothers that had sold him into slavery in the first place. But his brothers were still afraid he would seek retribution. And Joseph told them, "You intended to harm me, but God intended it for good to accomplish what is now being done, the saving of many lives."

God does turn evil things into good things. And it is our faith in remembering these things that can help us when we are feeling hopeless. And, as with Joseph, it may take time. Waiting can be so difficult. The world we live in today has conditioned us for instant gratification. I feel this microwave, stream-on-demand conditioning has made us very intolerant to waiting, and from there, it is just a small step to feeling hopeless. Personally, I struggle with patience. I want what I want, and I want it now! I have heard it joked not to ask God for patience, as He will put you in a situation to teach you patience. But we must have patience, my friends. God will come through. He always does. Maybe not in the way or in the time that you wanted, but He knows what and when is best.

Not only so, but we also glory in our sufferings, because we know that suffering produces perseverance; perseverance, character; and character, hope.

Romans 5:4–5 NIV

And hope, my friends, is the opposite of hopelessness.

If you struggle with feelings of hopelessness and despair, you may want to seek Christian counseling or a Christian support group to help you.

The Psalms are filled with beautiful writings of feelings of despair and calling and waiting on God to overcome them by having faith in what He has already done. One of my favorites is Psalm 77, and I encourage you to read it, pray it, and meditate on it when you are feeling hopeless. For me, the verses in Psalm 77 that help me are these:

I will remember the deeds of the LORD; yes, I will remember your miracles of long ago. I will consider all your works and meditate on all your mighty deeds.

Psalm 77:11–12 NIV

Let's look at some other Scripture that can help us with feelings of hopelessness and despair.

Praise be to the God and Father of our Lord Jesus Christ, the Father of compassion and the God of all comfort, who comforts us in all our troubles, so that we can comfort those in any trouble with the comfort we ourselves receive from God.

2 Corinthians 1:3–4 NIV

Therefore we do not lose heart. Though outwardly we are wasting away, yet inwardly we are being renewed day by day. For our light and momentary troubles are achieving for us an eternal glory that far outweighs them all.

2 Corinthians 4:16–17 NIV

Who shall separate us from the love of Christ? Shall trouble or hardship or persecution or famine or nakedness or danger or sword?

Romans 8:35 NIV

And we know that in all things God works for the good of those who love him, who are called according to his purpose.

Romans 8:28 NIV

> *Wait for the LORD; be strong and take heart and wait for the LORD.*
>
> Psalm 27:14 NIV

And once more, let's work on a prayer. You can use these or other verses to build your prayer.

Heavenly Father, Lord Jesus, Holy Spirit—

I come to You today seeking union with You, God. I praise You for who You are—God Almighty! The creator of the heavens and the earth. The creator of me. I was created in Your image, and You bless me (Genesis 1:27–28). You created my inmost being. You knit me together in my mother's womb, and I am fearfully and wonderfully made. I know that Your works are wonderful (Psalm 139:13–14).

Heavenly Father, Lord Jesus, Holy Spirit, I am under attack. I ask You for Your guidance and strength. Fill me with Your Holy Spirit, God, and give me Your strength to resist, rebuke, and fight these attacks.

Lord Jesus, I am feeling hopeless. I am filled with despair. But the Spirit You give me gives me power, love, and self-discipline (2 Timothy 1:7). Holy Spirit, fill me today. You are always with me. You are power, love, and self-discipline to conquer hopelessness. I release all hopelessness and despair to You, God. (Describe the situation that is making you feel hopeless.) Jesus, I invite You into my troubled heart. Meet me here, Jesus.

Heavenly Father, You are the Father of compassion and the God of all comfort. God, I ask for Your comfort today. Jesus, let what I am experiencing now and the comfort I receive from You be of comfort to others (2 Corinthians 1:3-4).

Lord Jesus, help me not to lose heart. Renew me, Jesus, for I know that this is temporary. I know that my future is glorious with You (2 Corinthians 4:16-17).

Jesus, I know nothing can separate me from Your love. Jesus, fill me with Your love today (Romans 8:35).

God, I know that You work all things for good for those who love You. God, I do love You, and this is for Your purpose, and I trust You (Romans 8:28).

LORD, I will wait for You to see me through this trouble, as I know You will. Strengthen me as I wait for You, God (Psalms 27:14).

Almighty God, may all this be accomplished now by You and through the mighty name of my Lord and Savior, Jesus Christ. I give You all glory, honor, thanks, and praise.

I love You, I trust You, and I worship You.

In Jesus' name, I pray,

Amen.

And once more, let's rebuke hopelessness. Use these or verses of your choosing.

God created me and formed me in His image and blesses me, for it is written, *"So God created mankind in his own image, in the image of God he created them; male and female he created them. God blessed them and said to them, 'Be fruitful and increase in number; fill the earth and subdue it'"* (Genesis 1:27–28 NIV).

God created me and knows me, and I am wonderfully made, for it is written, *"For you created my inmost being; you knit me together in my mother's womb. I praise you because I am fearfully and wonderfully made; your works are wonderful, I know that full well"* (Psalm 139:13–14 NIV).

I believe Jesus Christ is the Son of God. He is my Lord and Savior. I am a child of God, and I belong to Him, for it is written, *"Yet to all who did receive him, to those who believed in his name, he gave the right to become children of God"* (John 1:12 NIV).

In the name and in the authority of my Lord and Savior Jesus Christ, and by and through the Holy Spirit, I now use the three-strand cord of God from Ecclesiastes to bind up all spirits of hopelessness and despair that are attacking me now, for it is written, *"A cord of three strands is not quickly broken"* (Ecclesiastes 4:12 NIV).

In the name and in the authority of my Lord and Savior Jesus Christ, I command you bound, tied up, and rendered useless, for it is written, *"How can anyone enter a strong man's house and carry off his possessions unless he first ties up the strong man? Then he can plunder his house"* (Matthew 12:29 NIV).

All authority in heaven and on earth has been given to Jesus, for Jesus said of Himself, and it is written, *"All authority in heaven and on earth has been given to me"* (Matthew 28:18 NIV).

The name of Jesus is above all names, for it is written, *"Therefore God exalted him to the highest place and gave him the name that is above every name, that at the name of Jesus every knee should bow, in heaven and on earth and under the earth, and every tongue acknowledge that Jesus Christ is Lord, to the glory of God the Father"* (Philippians 2:9–11 NIV).

I command all spirits of hopelessness and despair tied up and bound in the name and in the authority of my Lord and Savior, Jesus Christ, and you must submit to Him and His authority.

The Spirit of God is in me, and the Holy Spirit does not make me hopeless but gives me hope. The Holy Spirit gives me power, love, and self-discipline, for it is written, *"For the Spirit God gave us does not make us timid, but gives us power, love and self-discipline"* (2 Timothy 1:7 NIV).

God is compassionate and comforts me in all my times of trouble, for it is written, *"Praise be to the God and Father of our Lord Jesus Christ, the Father of compassion and the God of all comfort, who comforts us in all our troubles, so that we can comfort those in any trouble with the comfort we ourselves receive from God"* (2 Corinthians 1:3–4 NIV). I belong to God, and He loves me.

I do not lose heart, as I am being renewed by God every day. This is temporary; this trouble brings me an eternal glory that outweighs this, for it is written, *"Therefore we do not lose heart. Though outwardly we are wasting away, yet inwardly we are being renewed day by day. For our light and momentary troubles are achieving for us an eternal glory that far outweighs them all"* (2 Corinthians 4:16–17 NIV).

I will not be hopeless because no trouble can separate me from the love of my Lord and Savior, Jesus Christ, for it is written, *"Who shall separate us from the love of Christ? Shall trouble or hardship or persecution or famine or nakedness or danger or sword?"* (Romans 8:35 NIV).

God works all things for good for those who love him, for it is written, *"And we know that in all things God works for the good of those who love him, who are called according to his purpose*" (Romans 8:28 NIV). I love God. I belong to Him.

I will be strong in the spirit, take heart, and wait for the LORD, for it is written, "*Wait for the LORD; be strong and take heart and wait for the LORD*" (Psalms 27:14 NIV).

In the name and in the authority of my Lord and Savior Jesus Christ, and by and through the Holy Spirit, I declare all demonic strongholds of hopelessness and despair demolished, for it is written, "*For though we live in the world, we do not wage war as the world does. The weapons we fight with are not the weapons of the world. On the contrary, they have divine power to demolish strongholds*" (2 Corinthians 10:4 NIV).

In the name and in the authority of my Lord and Savior Jesus Christ and by and through the Holy Spirit, I now command all spirits of hopelessness and despair to leave me. All spirits of hopelessness and despair, all backups and replacements, all weapons and devices, for it is written, "'*No weapon forged against you will prevail, and you will refute every tongue that accuses you. This is the heritage of the servants of the LORD, and this is their vindication from me,*' *declares the LORD*" (Isaiah 54:17 NIV).

In the name and in the authority of my Lord and Savior Jesus Christ, I now banish all spirits of hopelessness and despair from me and command you bound to the feet of Jesus for judgment with the three-strand cord of God, for it is written, "*Depart from me, you who are cursed, into the eternal fire prepared for the devil and his angels*" (Matthew 25:41 NIV).

And we finish with prayer.

Almighty God, may all this be accomplished now by You and through the mighty name of my Lord and Savior, Jesus Christ. I give You all glory, honor, thanks, and praise. I love You, I trust You, and I worship You. Jesus, I ask this in Your name,

Amen.

When things don't happen as we expect them to or in our timeframe, it can sometimes lead to feelings of hopelessness and despair. Stay strong and resilient because, as was the case with Joseph, there may be a much bigger plan that you aren't seeing yet.

We have come quite a long way on this journey, and you are doing great! But if there are still things going on that have you confused, we will cover that next.

CHAPTER 15

How We Fight
Confusion

Confusion is another tactic of the devil and a powerful one. As with other attacks, confusion can hinder us and render us ineffective. It is important to understand that the devil deceives. This deceit can cause tremendous confusion.

Google defines confusion as a lack of understanding; or uncertainty.[28] So when we are confused, uncertain, and without understanding, we should seek certainty and understanding. We should seek wisdom.

The entire Book of Proverbs is a great source of Scripture on wisdom, specifically Proverbs Chapters 1–9. There is much wisdom to be found in Psalms as well. I encourage you to explore further and meditate on both Psalms and Proverbs. But for now, let's look at some other scriptures that address seeking wisdom to help overcome confusion.

> *If any of you lacks wisdom, you should ask God, who gives generously to all without finding fault, and it will be given to you.*
>
> *James 1:5 NIV*

---

[28] Google's English Dictionary is provided by Oxford Languages.

> *For God is not a God of disorder but of peace—as in all the congregations of the Lord's people.*
>
> 1 Corinthians 14:33 NIV
>
> *But we have the mind of Christ.*
>
> 1 Corinthians 2:16 NIV
>
> *Give me understanding, so that I may keep your law and obey it with all my heart.*
>
> Psalm 119:34 NIV
>
> *Trust in the LORD with all your heart and lean not on your own understanding.*
>
> Proverbs 3:5 NIV
>
> *The mind governed by the flesh is death, but the mind governed by the Spirit is life and peace.*
>
> Romans 8:6 NIV
>
> *And no wonder, for Satan himself masquerades as an angel of light.*
>
> 2 Corinthians 11:14

Let's now work on a prayer to help us when we are feeling confused. Again, you can use some or all of these verses or choose verses that speak to you. Let the Holy Spirit guide you.

Heavenly Father, Lord Jesus, Holy Spirit—

I come to You today seeking union with You, God. I praise You for who You are—God Almighty! The creator of the heavens and the earth. The creator of me. I was created in Your image, and You bless me (Genesis 1:27–28). You created my inmost being. You knit me together in my mother's womb, and I am fearfully and wonderfully made. I know that Your works are wonderful (Psalm 139:13–14).

Heavenly Father, Lord Jesus, Holy Spirit, I am under attack. I ask You for Your guidance and strength. Fill me with Your Holy Spirit, God, and give me Your strength to resist, rebuke, and fight these attacks.

Lord Jesus, I am feeling confused. But the Spirit You give me gives me power, love, and self-discipline (2 Timothy 1:7). Holy Spirit, fill me today. You are always with me. You are power, love, and self-discipline to conquer confusion. I release all my confusion to You, God. (Describe the situation that is making you feel confused.)

Almighty God, I come to You today seeking wisdom. Please give me wisdom and discernment, for I am feeling confused. Give my mind rest, Jesus (James 1:5).

God, I know this confusion does not come from You, for You are not a God of disorder but of peace, and I belong to You (1 Corinthians 14:33).

Jesus, scripture tells me that I have the mind of Christ. Help me to be of one mind with You, Jesus. I receive Your mind with thanks (1 Corinthians 2:16).

God, please give me understanding today. Holy Spirit, speak to me and share with me Your Word (Psalm 119:34).

Lord, I trust in You with all my heart. Help me not to lean on my own understanding, but to trust in You and Your Word (Proverbs 3:5).

Holy Spirit, I consecrate my mind to You today. Come and fill my mind. Govern my mind. Fill my mind with life and peace (Romans 8:6).

Lord Jesus, I know that Satan masquerades as an angel of light and tries to confuse me. Please give me the wisdom and discernment to hear Your voice over his (2 Corinthians 11:14).

Almighty God, may all this be accomplished now by You and through the mighty name of my Lord and Savior, Jesus Christ. I give You all glory, honor, thanks, and praise.

I love You, I trust You, and I worship You.

In Jesus' name, I pray,

Amen.

Now to rebuke confusion. You now know the rhythm—use all or some of these verses, or choose your own.

God created me and formed me in His image and blesses me, for it is written, "*So God created mankind in his own image, in the image of God he created them; male and female he created them. God blessed them and said to them, 'Be fruitful and increase in number; fill the earth and subdue it'*" (Genesis 1:27–28 NIV).

God created me and knows me, and I am wonderfully made, for it is written, "*For you created my inmost being; you knit me together in my mother's womb. I praise you because I am fearfully and wonderfully made; your works are wonderful, I know that full well*" (Psalm 139:13–14 NIV).

I believe Jesus Christ is the Son of God. He is my Lord and Savior. I am a child of God, and I belong to Him, for it is written, "*Yet to all who did receive him, to those who believed in his name, he gave the right to become children of God*" (John 1:12 NIV).

In the name and in the authority of my Lord and Savior Jesus Christ, and by and through the Holy Spirit, I now use the three-strand cord of God from Ecclesiastes to bind up all spirits of confusion that are attacking me now, for it is written, "*A cord of three strands is not quickly broken*" (Ecclesiastes 4:12 NIV).

In the name and in the authority of my Lord and Savior Jesus Christ, I command you bound, tied up, and rendered useless, for it is written, "*How can anyone enter a strong man's house and carry off his possessions unless he first ties up the strong man? Then he can plunder his house*" (Matthew 12:29 NIV).

All authority in heaven and on earth has been given to Jesus, for Jesus said of Himself, and it is written, "*All authority in heaven and on earth has been given to me*" (Matthew 28:18 NIV).

The name of Jesus is above all names, for it is written, "*Therefore God exalted him to the highest place and gave him the name that is above every name, that at the name of Jesus every knee should bow, in heaven and on earth and under the earth, and every tongue acknowledge that Jesus Christ is Lord, to the glory of God the Father*" (Philippians 2:9–11 NIV).

I command all spirits of confusion tied up and bound in the name and in the authority of my Lord and Savior, Jesus Christ, and you must submit to Him and His authority.

The Spirit of God is in me, and the Holy Spirit does not make me confused but gives me wisdom. The Holy Spirit gives me power, love, and self-discipline, for it is written, *"For the Spirit God gave us does not make us timid, but gives us power, love and self-discipline"* (2 Timothy 1:7 NIV).

God generously gives me wisdom to overcome your confusion, for it is written, *"If any of you lacks wisdom, you should ask God, who gives generously to all without finding fault, and it will be given to you"* (James 1:5 NIV).

God is not a God of disorder, but a God of peace, and I belong to Him, for it is written, *"For God is not a God of disorder but of peace—as in all the congregations of the Lord's people"* (1 Corinthians 14:33 NIV).

I will not be confused because I have the mind of Christ, for it is written, *"But we have the mind of Christ"* (1 Corinthians 2:16 NIV).

I will not be confused because God gives me understanding so that I may keep His laws, for it is written, *"Give me understanding, so that I may keep your law and obey it with all my heart"* (Psalm 119:34 NIV).

I will not be confused because I trust in God with all my heart and lean on Him rather than my own understanding, for it is written, *"Trust in the LORD with all your heart and lean not on your own understanding"* (Proverbs 3:5 NIV).

I will not be confused because my mind is governed by the Holy Spirit of God, which brings me life and peace, for it is written, *"The mind governed by the flesh is death, but the mind governed by the Spirit is life and peace"* (Romans 8:6 NIV).

Satan, in the name and in the authority of my Lord and Savior Jesus Christ, I rebuke you from masquerading as an angel of light in my life, and you do not deceive me, for it is written, "*And no wonder, for Satan himself masquerades as an angel of light*" (2 Corinthians 11:14 NIV).

In the name and in the authority of my Lord and Savior Jesus Christ, and by and through the Holy Spirit, I declare all demonic strongholds of confusion demolished, for it is written, "*For though we live in the world, we do not wage war as the world does. The weapons we fight with are not the weapons of the world. On the contrary, they have divine power to demolish strongholds*" (2 Corinthians 10:4 NIV).

In the name and in the authority of my Lord and Savior Jesus Christ and by and through the Holy Spirit, I now command all spirits of confusion to leave me. All spirits of confusion, all backups and replacements, all weapons and devices, for it is written, "'*No weapon forged against you will prevail, and you will refute every tongue that accuses you. This is the heritage of the servants of the LORD, and this is their vindication from me,*' *declares the LORD*" (Isaiah 54:17 NIV).

In the name and in the authority of my Lord and Savior Jesus Christ, I now banish all spirits of confusion from me and command you bound to the feet of Jesus for judgment with the three-strand cord of God, for it is written, "*Depart from me, you who are cursed, into the eternal fire prepared for the devil and his angels*" (Matthew 25:41 NIV).

Once again, let's finish with a prayer.

Almighty God, may all this be accomplished now by You and through the mighty name of my Lord and Savior, Jesus Christ. I give You all glory, honor, thanks, and praise. I love You, I trust You, and I worship You. Jesus, I ask this in Your name,

Amen.

We have covered many of the common lies told to us by the devil in his plan to steal, kill, and destroy the full life that Jesus wants to give us. Now let's look at another form of attack that all of us face—temptation.

CHAPTER 16

How We Fight Temptation

While fear, worry, anxiety, feelings of loneliness and abandonment, hopelessness, and confusion can hinder many of us from time to time, I don't believe any of us are exempt from temptation, and it happens frequently. Even Jesus was tempted.

> *Then Jesus was led by the Spirit into the wilderness to be tempted by the devil.*
>
> Matthew 4:1 NIV

But did you catch that? Jesus was *led by the Spirit* into the wilderness to be tempted. Why would the Spirit of God lead the Son of God, who is God, into the wilderness to be tempted? Most biblical scholars believe that one reason was to show His humanity. The Bible does give us answers. Jesus is fully God but also fully human. God in human form. As the Apostle John puts it:

> *The Word became flesh and made his dwelling among us.*
>
> John 1:14 NIV

And the Book of Hebrews tells us this:

Therefore, since we have a great high priest who has ascended into heaven, Jesus the Son of God, let us hold firmly to the faith we profess. For we do not have a high priest who is unable to empathize with our weaknesses, but we have one who has been tempted in every way, just as we are—yet he did not sin. Let us then approach God's throne of grace with confidence, so that we may receive mercy and find grace to help us in our time of need.

Hebrews 4:14-16 NIV

Jesus had to show us His humanity. By doing this, He set the example for us to follow.

We are all tempted, and we are all tempted in different ways. The Apostle John breaks down the different kinds of temptation for us:

For everything in the world—the lust of the flesh, the lust of the eyes, and the pride of life—comes not from the Father but from the world.

1 John 2:16 NIV

And we know from Chapter 9 that Jesus Himself called the devil *"the prince of this world."* We live in this world, so temptations are all around us. For some, the lust of the flesh will be the one they struggle with the most. For others, the lust of the eyes, and for others, the pride of life. But we all more than likely struggle with all of them at different times. And we all give in to sin from time to time. We all sin. But we always have a way out. We can overcome sin. And when we do sin, we need to quickly confess this sin to God and repent.

Since we will all be tempted differently at different times, if there is a particular sin you are struggling with, find Scripture that addresses it. Use it in your prayers and in your rebukes. If your temptations have led to addiction, I encourage you to seek guidance from a Christian counselor or a Christian support group.

Here are some scriptures about temptation:

> *No temptation has overtaken you except what is common to mankind. And God is faithful; he will not let you be tempted beyond what you can bear. But when you are tempted, he will also provide you a way out so you can endure it.*
>
> 1 Corinthians 10:13 NIV

> *So I say, walk by the Spirit, and you will not gratify the desires of the flesh.*
>
> Galatians 5:16–17 NIV

> *If you love me, keep my commands.*
>
> John 14:15 NIV

> *Submit yourselves then, to God. Resist the devil, and he will flee from you.*
>
> James 4:7 NIV

> *Jesus said to him, "Away from me Satan! For it is written: 'Worship the Lord your God, and serve him only.'"*
>
> Matthew 4:10 NIV

Ok, you know where we are headed next. Let's work on a prayer for resisting temptation.

Heavenly Father, Lord Jesus, Holy Spirit—

I come to You today seeking union with You, God. I praise You for who You are—God Almighty! The creator of the heavens and the earth. The creator of me. I was created in Your image, and You bless me (Genesis 1:27–28). You created my inmost being. You knit me together in my mother's womb, and I am fearfully and wonderfully made. I know that Your works are wonderful (Psalm 139:13–14).

Heavenly Father, Lord Jesus, Holy Spirit, I am under attack. I ask You for Your guidance and strength. Fill me with Your Holy Spirit, God, and give me Your strength to resist, rebuke, and fight these attacks.

Lord Jesus, I am being tempted. But the Spirit You give me gives me power, love, and self-discipline (2 Timothy 1:7). Holy Spirit, fill me today. You are always with me. You are power, love, and self-discipline to conquer temptation. I release all my temptation to You, God. (Describe the situation and how you are being tempted.)

God, do not let this temptation overtake me. You are faithful. God, I ask that You provide a way and lead me out of this temptation so I can endure it (1 Corinthians 10:13).

Holy Spirit, fill me and be with me today. Walk with me to overcome the desires of the flesh (Galatians 5:16–17).

Lord Jesus, I love You. I can do all things through You, as You give me strength. Give me the strength to keep Your commands, Jesus (John 14:15 and Philippians 4:13).

Almighty God, I submit myself to You today and every day to resist the devil. When I resist him, he will flee from me (James 4:7).

I worship You, God, and serve You only (Matthew 4:10).

I release all my temptation to You, Jesus. Meet me here in this place of temptation, and give me Your strength. Provide a way out for me.

Almighty God, may all this be accomplished now by You and through the mighty name of my Lord and Savior, Jesus Christ. I give You all glory, honor, thanks, and praise.

I love You, I trust You, and I worship You.

In Jesus' name, I pray,

Amen.

Now let's rebuke temptation.

God created me and formed me in His image and blesses me, for it is written, "*So God created mankind in his own image, in the image of God he created them; male and female he created them. God blessed them and said to them, 'Be fruitful and increase in number; fill the earth and subdue it'*" (Genesis 1:27–28 NIV).

God created me and knows me, and I am wonderfully made, for it is written, "*For you created my inmost being; you* knit me together in my mother's womb. I praise you because I am fearfully and wonderfully made; your works are wonderful, I know that full well" (Psalm 139:13–14 NIV).

I believe Jesus Christ is the Son of God. He is my Lord and Savior. I am a child of God, and I belong to Him, for it is written, "*Yet to all who did receive him, to those who believed in his name, he gave the right to become children of God*" (John 1:12 NIV).

In the name and in the authority of my Lord and Savior Jesus Christ, and by and through the Holy Spirit, I now use the three-strand cord of God from Ecclesiastes to bind up all spirits of temptation that are attacking me now, for it is written, "*A cord of three strands is not quickly broken*" (Ecclesiastes 4:12 NIV).

In the name and in the authority of my Lord and Savior Jesus Christ, I command you bound, tied up, and rendered useless, for it is written, "*How can anyone enter a strong man's house and carry off his possessions unless he first ties up the strong man? Then he can plunder his house*" (Matthew 12:29 NIV).

All authority in heaven and on earth has been given to Jesus, for Jesus said of Himself, and it is written, "*All authority in heaven and on earth has been given to me*" (Matthew 28:18 NIV).

The name of Jesus is above all names, for it is written, "*Therefore God exalted him to the highest place and gave him the name that is above every name, that at the name of Jesus every knee should bow, in heaven and on earth and under the earth, and every tongue acknowledge that Jesus Christ is Lord, to the glory of God the Father*" (Philippians 2:9–11 NIV).

I command all spirits of temptation tied up and bound in the name and in the authority of my Lord and Savior, Jesus Christ, and you must submit to Him and His authority.

The Spirit of God is in me, and the Holy Spirit does not tempt me. The Holy Spirit gives me power, love, and self-discipline to conquer temptation, for it is written, "*For the Spirit God gave us does not make us timid, but gives us power, love and self-discipline*" (2 Timothy 1:7 NIV).

I will not let temptation overtake me. God is faithful and provides a way out for me, for it is written, "*No temptation has overtaken you except what is common to mankind. And God is faithful; he will not let you be tempted beyond what you can bear. But when you are tempted, he will also provide you a way out so you can endure it*" (1 Corinthians 10:13 NIV).

The Spirit of God in me walks with me, and I will not gratify the desires of the flesh, for it is written, "*So I say, walk by the Spirit, and you will not gratify the desires of the flesh*" (Galatians 5:16–17 NIV).

I love my Lord and Savior Jesus Christ and will obey His commands, for Jesus said, and it is written, "*If you love me, keep my commands*" (John 14:15 NIV).

I submit myself to God, I resist temptation, and I command you to flee! For it is written, "*Submit yourselves then, to God. Resist the devil, and he will flee from you*" (James 4:7 NIV).

In the name and in the authority of my Lord and Savior, Jesus Christ, I command you away from me, Satan! I worship the Lord God and serve Him only, for it is written, "*Jesus said to him, 'Away from me Satan!' For it is written: 'Worship the Lord your God, and serve him only'*" (Matthew 4:10 NIV).

In the name and in the authority of my Lord Jesus Christ, and by and through the Holy Spirit, I declare all demonic strongholds of temptation demolished, for it is written, "*For though we live in the world, we do not wage war as the world does. The weapons we fight with are not the weapons of the world. On the contrary, they have divine power to demolish strongholds*" (2 Corinthians 10:3–4 NIV).

In the name and in the authority of my Lord Jesus Christ and by and through the Holy Spirit, I now command all spirits of temptation to leave me. You and all backups and replacements, all weapons and devices. No weapon formed against me will prevail, and I refute your accusations, for it is written, "'*No weapon forged against you will prevail, and you will refute every tongue that accuses you. This is the heritage of the servants of the LORD, and this is their vindication from me,' declares the LORD*" (Isaiah 54:17 NIV). In the name and in the authority of my Lord and Savior, Jesus Christ, I now command you bound to the feet of Jesus for judgment with the three-strand cord of God.

Once again, let's finish with a prayer.

Almighty God, may all this be accomplished now by You and through the mighty name of my Lord and Savior, Jesus Christ. I give You all glory, honor, thanks, and praise. I love You, I trust You, and I worship You. Jesus, I ask this in Your name,

Amen.

Great job, my friends! We have gone through preparing ourselves and exploring how we can resist the forces of evil when we are under attack. But what about helping others when they may be under attack? Let's keep going!

CHAPTER 17

How We Fight
Fighting for Others

Let's look at some examples from the Bible of demonic possession and how the demons were driven out. And the first place we should always look is to Jesus.

They sailed to the region of the Gerasenes, which is across the lake from Galilee. When Jesus stepped ashore, he was met by a demon-possessed man from the town. For a long time this man had not worn clothes or lived in a house, but had lived in the tombs. When he saw Jesus, he cried out and fell at his feet, shouting at the top of his voice, "What do you want with me, Jesus, Son of the Most High God? I beg you, don't torture me!" For Jesus had commanded the impure spirit to come out of the man. Many times it had seized him, and though he was chained hand and foot and kept under guard, he had broken the chains and had been driven by the demon into solitary places.

Jesus asked him, "What is your name?"

"Legion," he replied, because many demons had gone into him. And they begged Jesus repeatedly not to order them to go to the Abyss.

> *A large herd of pigs was feeding there on the hillside. The demons begged Jesus to let them go into the pigs, and he gave them permission. When the demons came out of the man, they went into the pigs, and the herd rushed down the steep bank into the lake and was drowned.*
>
> Luke 8:26–33 NIV

We see here that Jesus commanded the impure spirits to come out of the man, and they obeyed. The impure spirits also knew who Jesus was. They begged Him not to send them to the Abyss. They know His power and authority.

> *They went to Capernaum, and when the Sabbath came, Jesus went into the synagogue and began to teach. The people were amazed at his teaching, because he taught them as one who had authority, not as the teachers of the law. Just then a man in their synagogue who was possessed by an impure spirit cried out, "What do you want with us, Jesus of Nazareth? Have you come to destroy us? I know who you are—the Holy One of God!"*
>
> *"Be quiet!" Jesus said sternly. "Come out of him!"*
>
> *The impure spirit shook the man violently and came out of him with a shriek.*
>
> Mark 1:21–26 NIV

Again, the spirit recognized Jesus and knew who He was and knew He had the power and the authority to destroy them. Jesus spoke sternly to the spirit and commanded him to come out of the man.

There are other examples of Jesus driving out demons in Scripture, but I chose these in order to highlight that the demonic forces know who Jesus is, and they know His power and authority. I also chose these to show that Jesus commanded these spirits out and, in the case of the man in the synagogue, spoke sternly to the spirit. In both cases, Jesus did not ask. Jesus commanded.

In the Book of Acts, Luke describes how Paul commands a spirit out of a girl.

> *Once when we were going to the place of prayer, we were met by a female slave who had a spirit by which she predicted the future. She earned a great deal of money for her owners by fortune-telling. She followed Paul and the rest of us, shouting, "These men are servants of the Most High God, who are telling you the way to be saved." She kept this up for many days. Finally Paul became so annoyed that he turned around and said to the spirit, "In the name of Jesus Christ I command you to come out of her!" At that moment the spirit left her.*
>
> *Acts 16:16–18 NIV*

Paul commanded the spirit to come out of the girl, but he commanded it in the name of Jesus Christ.

Again, these are biblical examples of demonic possession. As Christians, we can be oppressed by an evil spirit. We cannot be demon-possessed. But unfortunately, non-believers can be demon possessed. It is not just something in the movies. It happens. Scripture tells us it happens. It happened then, and it is happening today. You may be called on at some time to help in a situation of demon possession. Or to help a brother or sister in Christ who is being oppressed. So, how do you approach this?

It's very similar to the prayer and rebuking that we did earlier. We are interceding in prayer for another person and directing the rebukes at the demonic spirits, but in this case, they are spirits that are oppressing or possessing someone else. If you are interceding in prayer for or rebuking for a follower of Christ, you may choose to include them in your prayer and rebuke.

The very first thing you need to do is protect yourself. Again, make sure there is no unconfessed sin in your life or unforgiveness in your heart. Then say aloud:

In the name and in the authority of my Lord Jesus Christ and by and through the Holy Spirit, I now bring the blood and cross of our Lord Jesus Christ between me and (name the person). I bring the full authority of our Lord Jesus Christ and the full work of Christ between me and (name the person)—their spirit, soul, and body, their sin, warfare, and corruption. I send every human spirit bound back to (name the person)'s body. I command all their sin, warfare, and corruption bound back to the work of Christ in their life, and I forbid it to transfer to me.[29]

Then a prayer of protection for yourself:

Almighty God, I ask that You Yourself be a fiery wall of love and protection around me. May Your glory be found within (Zechariah 3:5). Almighty God, may all this be accomplished now by You and in the name and in the authority of my Lord Jesus Christ and by and through the Holy Spirit. God, I give You all glory, honor,

---

[29] Adapted from John Eldredge.

thanks, and praise. I love You, I trust You, and I worship You. I ask this in Jesus' name. Amen.

You can then proceed to rebuke the spirit of possession as we did the spirit of oppression. Remember, you are not asking. You should be stern. You are commanding in the name of Jesus.

God created (name the person) and me and formed us in His image and blesses us, for it is written, "*So God created mankind in his own image, in the image of God he created them; male and female he created them. God blessed them and said to them, 'Be fruitful and increase in number; fill the earth and subdue it'*" (Genesis 1:27–28 NIV).

God created (name the person) and me and knows us, and we are wonderfully made, for it is written, "*For you created my inmost being; you knit me together in my mother's womb. I praise you because I am fearfully and wonderfully made; your works are wonderful, I know that full well*" (Psalm 139:13–14 NIV).

I believe Jesus Christ is the Son of God. (If the person is a believer, include them as well.) He is my (or our) Lord and Savior. I (or we) am (or are) a child (or children) of God, and I (or we) belong to Him, for it is written, "*Yet to all who did receive him, to those who believed in his name, he gave the right to become children of God*" (John 1:12 NIV).

In the name and in the authority of my (or our) Lord and Savior Jesus Christ, and by and through the Holy Spirit, I (or we) now use the three-strand cord of God from Ecclesiastes to bind up all spirits of (name the type of attack) that are attacking (name the person) now, for it is written, "*A cord of three strands is not quickly broken*" (Ecclesiastes 4:12 NIV).

In the name and in the authority of my Lord and Savior Jesus Christ, I (or we) command you bound, tied up, and rendered useless, for it is written, "*How can anyone enter a strong man's house and carry off his possessions unless he first ties up the strong man? Then he can plunder his house*" (Matthew 12:29 NIV).

All authority in heaven and on earth has been given to Jesus, for Jesus said of Himself, and it is written, "*All authority in heaven and on earth has been given to me*" (Matthew 28:18 NIV).

The name of Jesus is above all names, for it is written, "*Therefore God exalted him to the highest place and gave him the name that is above every name, that at the name of Jesus every knee should bow, in heaven and on earth and under the earth, and every tongue acknowledge that Jesus Christ is Lord, to the glory of God the Father*" (Philippians 2:9–11 NIV).

I (or we) command all spirits attacking (name the person) tied up and bound in the name and in the authority of my (or our) Lord and Savior Jesus Christ, and you must submit to Him and His authority.

The Spirit of God is in me (or us). The Holy Spirit gives me (or us) power, love and self-discipline to conquer, for it is written, "*For the Spirit God gave us does not make us timid, but gives us power, love and self-discipline*" (2 Timothy 1:7 NIV).

In the name and in the authority of my (or our) Lord Jesus Christ, and by and through the Holy Spirit, I (or we) declare all demonic strongholds demolished, for it is written, "*For though we live in the world, we do not wage war as the world does. The weapons we fight with are not the weapons of the world. On the contrary, they have divine power to demolish strongholds*" (2 Corinthians 10:3–4 NIV).

In the name and in the authority of my (or our) Lord Jesus Christ, and by and through the Holy Spirit, I (or we) command you to leave (name the person). You and all backups and replacements, all weapons and devices. No weapon formed against me (or us) will prevail, and I (or we) refute your accusations, for it is written, *"'No weapon forged against you will prevail, and you will refute every tongue that accuses you. This is the heritage of the servants of the LORD, and this is their vindication from me,' declares the LORD"* (Isaiah 54:17 NIV).

In the name and in the authority of my (or our) Lord and Savior Jesus Christ, I (or we) now banish all demonic spirits from (name the person) and command you bound to the feet of Jesus for judgment with the three-strand cord of God, for it is written, *"Depart from me, you who are cursed, into the eternal fire prepared for the devil and his angels"* (Matthew 25:41 NIV).

And we finish with prayer.

Almighty God, I ask that You Yourself be a fiery wall of love and protection around (name the person) and me. May Your glory be found within (name the person) and me. Almighty God, may all this be accomplished now by You and in the name and in the authority of my (or our) Lord Jesus Christ and by and through the Holy Spirit. God, I give You all glory, honor, thanks, and praise. I love You, I trust You, and I worship You. I ask this in Jesus' name.

Amen.

I want to again stress the importance of being in a right place with God before interceding for others. Having unconfessed sin or unforgiveness in your heart will make you a target for these evil forces as well. And never forget to bring the full work of Christ between you and the other person, as well as the prayer of protection for yourself before you begin.

We've covered so much! Well done! So ... what comes next? Everything should be smooth sailing, right? Let's look at what we can expect.

CHAPTER 18

What to Expect

Congratulations, friends! You have made it through all the preparations and have seen examples of how to fight. Well done! Maybe you got this book because you were experiencing some sort of attack. I hope and pray that it has been helpful.

So, what comes next?

There Will Be Trouble

> *I have told you these things, so that in me you may have peace. In this world you will have trouble. But take heart! I have overcome the world.*
>
> *John 16:33 NIV*
>
> *Be very careful, then, how you live—not as unwise but as wise, making the most of every opportunity, because the days are evil.*
>
> *Ephesians 5:15-16 NIV*

Before we go any further, let's dispel some myths.

Some people think that as followers of Christ, we should not have any trouble. That God will allow nothing terrible to happen to us.

Jesus Himself tells us in the Book of Matthew—

> *Come to me, all you who are weary and burdened, and I will give you rest. Take my yoke and learn from me, for I am gentle and humble in heart, and you will find rest for your souls. For my yoke is easy and my burden is light.*
>
> Matthew 11:28–30 NIV

But wait, in the Book of John, Jesus says we will have trouble. Then which is true?

They are both true. In the world, there will be trouble. But even in difficult times, we can have peace in Jesus. Jesus has overcome the world, and in Him, we can find rest for our souls. In addition to taking His yoke, He also tells us to learn from Him. What do we learn from Jesus? Well, Jesus Himself gives us the two most important things for us to do.

> *Hearing that Jesus had silenced the Sadducees, the Pharisees got together. One of them, an expert in the law, tested him with this question: "Teacher, which is the greatest commandment of the Law?"*
>
> *Jesus replied: "Love the Lord your God with all your heart and with all your soul and with all your mind. This is the first and greatest commandment. And the second is like it: Love your neighbor as yourself. All the Law and the Prophets hang on these two commandments."*
>
> Matthew 22:34–40 NIV

Loving God and loving others? This really isn't a heavy burden Jesus is placing on us. Love? How hard can that be? Oh, but we do make it hard! Sometimes, others make it seem impossible to love them. And, if we really stop and do some deep self-reflection, sometimes we make it seem impossible for others to love us, too. Add on top that Satan is the prince of this world, and he has waged war on us, then, so, in this world, we will have trouble.

In all this rejoice, though now for a little while you may have had to suffer grief in all kinds of trials. These have come so that the proven genuineness of your faith—of greater worth than gold, which perishes even though refined by fire—may result in praise, glory, and honor when Jesus Christ is revealed.

1 Peter 1:6–7 NIV

Not only so, but we also glory in our sufferings, because we know that suffering produces perseverance, perseverance, character, and character, hope. And hope does not put us to shame, because God's love has been poured out into our hearts through the Holy Spirit, who has been given to us.

Romans 5:3–5 NIV

Now if we are children, then we are heirs—heirs of God and co-heirs with Christ, if indeed we share in his sufferings in order that we may also share in his glory.

Romans 8:17 NIV

Both the passage from 1 Peter and the passages from Romans tell us to expect suffering. But they also both tell us there is a benefit from our suffering. They prove and strengthen our faith if we lean on God during times of suffering, and they help us to persevere, build our character, and actually give us hope if we trust in God. Our suffering allows us to share in Christ's glory.

> *Enter through the narrow gate. For wide is the gate and broad is the road that leads to destruction, and many enter through it. But small is the gate and narrow is the road that leads to life, and only a few find it.*
>
> Matthew 7:13–14 NIV

As Christians, we will often be going against the majority. This can be lonely at times and can make us feel isolated. It is important to have Christian brothers and sisters whom we can gather with, share with, and confide in.

> *And let us consider how we may spur one another on toward love and good deeds, not giving up meeting together as some are in the habit of doing, but encouraging one another—and all the more as you see the day approaching.*
>
> Hebrews 10:24–25 NIV

So, my friends, do not expect smooth sailing at all times. There will be storms. But we can be content in seasons of trouble.

> *I know what it is to be in need, and I know what it is to have plenty. I have learned the secret of being content in any and every situation, whether well*

> *fed or hungry, whether living in plenty or in want. I can do all this through him who gives me strength.*
>
> *Philippians 4:12–13 NIV*

Remember, Paul wrote this *from prison*. He was not only content but providing encouragement to others as well.

And let's not forget Job. He was a righteous man, and the devil turned his life upside down. And God allowed it. Remember, the devil is powerful. He is the prince of this world, but he is no match for Jesus. All authority belongs to Jesus. We also learn from Job that Satan also can't do anything that God doesn't allow. We can see from the verses above that God allows trouble in our lives to grow us in faith. To build our character. But mostly to give us opportunities to fully trust in Him.

So, the truth is we will have trouble. Expect it. But we know now how better to align ourselves with God to prepare for it and how to rebuke it when it happens.

> *If you hold to my teaching, you really are my disciples. Then you will know the truth, and the truth will set you free.*
>
> *John 8:31–32 NIV*

Do not let disappointments discourage you. Do not put your hopes in the things or people of the world. They will always disappoint, then the evil one will always try to bring discouragement and despair.

> *He will speak against the Most High and will oppress his holy people.*
>
> *Daniel 7:25 NIV*

Let's look at that in another translation—

He shall speak words against the Most High, and shall wear out the saints of the Most High.

Daniel 7:25 ESV

The devil is relentless. He will try to wear you down. But we do not have to be discouraged! We have all we need in Jesus to stay strong.

Let us not become weary in doing good, for at the proper time we will reap a harvest if we do not give up.

Galatians 6:9 NIV

I'd like to recommend some additional resources for you. I have mentioned John Eldredge several times throughout this book. For you men out there, I highly recommend his book *Wild at Heart: Discovering the Secret of a Man's Soul*. He also has excellent resources available on his website at https://wildatheart.org/

John and his wife, Staci, also have a book specifically for women called *Captivating: Unveiling the Mystery of a Woman's Soul*.

John Eckhardt has a powerful book called *Prayers that Rout Demons*. It is full of scripture-based prayers and rebukes.

I also recommend and encourage you to download the companion workbook for this book. You can find it at www.zoelifeconsultinggroup.com.

Remember Elijah

Elijah prayed for it to rain, but it didn't happen right away. Elijah prayed seven times before his servant saw a small cloud. But Elijah didn't give up. He kept praying as we must keep praying and rebuking. These spirits are evil. They are disobedient. They may not go easily. Keep praying and keep rebuking.

God fights with us. Fights for us. As followers of Christ, The Holy Spirit lives in us to help us, strengthen us, and guide us. Again, Jesus said:

> *The thief comes only to steal and kill*
> *and destroy; I have come that they may*
> *have life, and have it to the full.*
>
> *John 10:10 NIV*

And if you aren't a follower of Christ? You can have the fullness of Christ too! Given from the grace, mercy, and unconditional love of God the Father. The offer is free and is for everyone. That's right—everyone. Even you. God loves you so much that he sent His Son Jesus here to earth to take away the sin of the whole world. All of humanity. We are all created in God's image, and He loves each and every one of us and came for all of us.

> *For God so loved the world that he gave his*
> *one and only Son, that whoever believes in*
> *him shall not perish but have eternal life.*
>
> *John 3:16 NIV*

The Spirit of the Lord is on me, because he has anointed me to proclaim good news to the poor. He has sent me to proclaim freedom for the prisoners and recovery of sight for the blind, to set the oppressed free, to proclaim the year of the Lord's favor.

Luke 4:18–19 NIV

Then Jesus came to them and said, "All authority in heaven and on earth has been given to me. Therefore go and make disciples of all nations, baptizing them in the name of the Father and of the Son and of the Holy Spirit, and teaching them to obey everything I have commanded you. And surely I am with you always, to the very end of the age."

Matthew 28:18–20 NIV

Jesus answered, "I am the way and the truth and the life. No one comes to the Father except through me."

John 14:6 NIV

On the last and greatest day of the festival, Jesus stood and said in a loud voice, "Let anyone who is thirsty come to me and drink. Whoever believes in me, as Scripture has said, rivers of living water will flow from within them."

John 7:37–38 NIV

Here I am! I stand at the door and knock. If anyone hears my voice and opens the door, I will come in and eat with that person, and they with me. To the one who is victorious, I will give the right to

> *sit with me on my throne, just as I was victorious and sat down with my Father on his throne.*
>
> Revelation 3:20–21 NIV

The offer is free and is for *everyone*, including you! If, in reading this book, something has sparked within you and made you yearn for more, you can have more than you ever imagined! Just say this simple prayer:

> *Jesus, I believe You are the Son of God. I believe that You died on the cross to rescue me from sin and eternal death. I believe that You were raised from the dead and now live eternally and that You offer this eternal life for me—for us to be together always. Jesus, I now ask You to take Your rightful place in my heart and in my life as my Lord and my Savior. Fill me with Your love and with Your life. Fill me with Your Holy Spirit to lead and guide me. Give me ears to hear You and eyes to see You as You teach me. Be a fiery wall of love and protection around me. Fill me with Your Glory.*
>
> *Jesus, I ask this in Your name.*
>
> *Amen.*

Thank you so much for taking the time to go through this book. My hopes and prayers are that this book has brought the light of Jesus into your life in some way and that you will look to Him always as the light in the darkness.

> *The people walking in darkness have seen a great light; on those living in the land of deep darkness a light has dawned.*
>
> Isaiah 9:2 NIV

The LORD bless you and keep you; the LORD make his face shine on you and be gracious to you; the LORD turn his face toward you and give you peace.

Numbers 6:24 NIV

God bless you, my friends.

ACKNOWLEDGMENTS

Glory, praise, honor, and thanks to my Heavenly Father, Lord Jesus, and The Holy Spirit for leading and guiding me throughout this process.

There are many people I need to thank as well—

Very special thanks to my wife, Minnie, for her mercy, grace, forgiveness, unconditional love, empathy, late nights, friendship, partnership, patience, invaluable insights, perspective, input, prayers, support, and encouragement. I couldn't have done this without you. I love you.

Thank you to my writing coach Scott Allen for his valuable insights and encouragement.

Thank you to my editor Sky Rodio Nuttall for her suggestions and guidance and for turning my manuscript into a book.

Thank you to Chandler Bolt and the entire team at SelfPublishing.com for the coaching, training, and support to make this book a reality.

Thank you to Dr. Jay Stigdon and Pastor Trent Renner for taking the time to read my rough draft and provide perspective and guidance.

Thank you to Pastor Mingo Palacios and the entire staff at Torrey Pines Church for timely and uplifting messages when I needed them.

Thank you to John Eldredge for your life-changing ministry, as well as for your guidance and prayers when I started this book-writing journey.

Thank you to my family and friends for your support and encouragement.

REVIEW

Can I ask a Favor?

Thank you for reading *Faith and the Fight—A Detailed Guide on Recognizing and Conquering Spiritual Attack in Everyday Life*!

I truly appreciate all your feedback, and I love hearing what you have to say.

I need your input to make the next version of this book and my future books better.

Please take two minutes now to leave a helpful review on Amazon, letting me know what you think of the book.

Thank you so much!

Michael Williams

ABOUT THE AUTHOR

Michael Williams is an author, consultant, and coach. He is a Certified Master Life Coach, holding Professional Life Coach, Life Purpose Coach, Goal Success Coach, and Happiness Coach certifications, and is a member of the International Christian Coaching Institute.

Prior to this, Michael spent many years in the IT industry, holding roles from hands-on technical to planning and strategic, managing and coaching teams along the way. He has held sales engineering and account executive roles as well.

Michael is a follower of Christ, loves Jesus, and loves reading, studying, and talking about the Bible and all things spiritual. His wife calls him her "Bible Wikipedia." Although he spends considerable time in Arizona, home is with his beautiful wife in Coronado, CA. Between Michael and his wife, they have six wonderful adult children (a regular Brady Bunch!) and two adorable grandchildren. Michael and his wife enjoy the beach life but also love getaways to the mountains. Michael loves cooking, and he can regularly be found in the kitchen or at the grill preparing something tasty. He has a life-long love of music and can fumble his way through a song or two on the drums.

NOTES

Chapter 1: What Is Spiritual Warfare?
1. *The Exorcist*, directed by William Friedkin, Warner Brothers, Hoya Productions, 1973.
2. *Lucifer*, developed by Tom Kapinos, Jerry Bruckheimer Television, DC Entertainment, Warner Bros. Television, Netflix, 2016–2021.

Chapter 2: Recognizing Spiritual Warfare
3. John Eldredge, *Wild at Heart Expanded Edition: Discovering the Secret of a Man's Soul*, Thomas Nelson, 2021.
4. C.S. Lewis, *The Screwtape Letters: Annotated Edition*, ed. Paul McCusker, Harper Collins, 2013.

Chapter 3: Preparing Yourself for the Fight—Union With God
5. YouVersion Bible App. Life.Church. Copyright 2008–2019.
6. One Minute Pause, Ransomed Heart Ministries, Copyright *Wild at Heart*.
7. John Eldredge, *Get Your Life Back*, Thomas Nelson, 2020.

Chapter 4: Preparing Yourself for the Fight—Sin, Repentance, Forgiveness, and Mercy
8. Daniel Doriani - www.biblestudytools.com/dictionary/sin
9. Google's English Dictionary is provided by Oxford Languages.
10. En.wikipedia.org/wiki/Repentance

Chapter 5: Preparing Yourself for the Fight—Faith, Trust, and the Holy Spirit
11. John and Staci Eldredge, *Love and War: Find Your Way to Something Beautiful in Your Marriage*, Waterbrook, 2011.

[12] John Eldredge, *All Things New: Heaven, Earth, and the Restoration of Everything You Love*, Thomas Nelson, 2018.

Chapter 6: Preparing Yourself for the Fight—Prayer and Fasting
[13] Thomas, N. Christian Fasting: Definition, Biblical Examples, & How-to. Retrieved from https://justdisciple.com/christian-fasting/
[14] Thomas, N. Christian Fasting: Definition, Biblical Examples, & How-to. Retrieved from https://justdisciple.com/christian-fasting/
[15] Thomas, N. Christian Fasting Rules, Guidelines, and Best Practices. Retrieved from https://justdisciple.com/fasting-rules/

Chapter 7: Preparing Yourself for the Fight—Understanding Your Authority

Chapter 8: Preparing Yourself for the Fight—The Armor of God
[16] *Married ... with Children*, created by Michael G. Moye, Ron Leavitt, Fox, 1987–1997.
[17] Google's English Dictionary is provided by Oxford Languages.
[18] https://www.britannica.com/topic/Gospel-New-Testament
[19] https://en.wikipedia.org/wiki/Rollen_Stewart

Chapter 9: Preparing Yourself for the Fight—Understanding the Enemy
[20] Sun Tzu, *The Art of War*, Filiquarian, 2007.
[21] Don Stewart, *Satan: Our Adversary the Devil*, EOW (Educating Our World), 2020.
[22] Don Stewart, *Satan: Our Adversary the Devil*, EOW (Educating Our World), 2020.

Chapter 10: How We Fight
[23] Google's English Dictionary is provided by Oxford Languages.
[24] Eldredge, John. *The Utter Relief of Holiness: How God's Goodness Frees Us From Everything that Plagues Us,* Thomas Nelson, 2003.

Chapter 11: How We Fight—Fear

Chapter 12: How We Fight—Worry and Anxiety
[25] Selby, S. 2018. What Is the Difference Between Sorry and Anxiety or Fear? Retrieved from https://www.sharonselby.com/anxiety/what-is-the-difference-between-worry-anxiety-and-fear
[26] LaFreniere, L. Newman, M. 2019. Retrieved from https://www.sciencedirect.com/science/article/abs/pii/S0005789419300826#

Chapter 13: How We Fight—Abandonment and Loneliness
[27] Mildes, E. 2020. 5 Practical Steps to Overcome Your Fear of Abandonment. Retrieved from https://seattlechristiancounseling.com/articles/5-practical-steps-to-overcome-your-fear-of-abandonment

Chapter 14: How We Fight—Hopelessness and Despair

Chapter 15: How We Fight—Confusion
[28] Google's English Dictionary is provided by Oxford Languages.

Chapter 16: How We Fight—Temptation

Chapter 17: How We Fight—Fighting for Others
[29] Adapted from John Eldredge.

Chapter 18: What to Expect

MORE

Thank you for reading this book! But finishing
this book is just the beginning…

Continue your journey at
www.zoelifeconsultinggroup.com

Made in United States
Orlando, FL
25 October 2023